FROM

MAGAZINE

Scale Modeling
TIPS AND TECHNIQUES

SCALE MODELING HANDBOOK NO. 12

Editor: Mark Hembree
Assistant Editor: Marcia Stern
Art Director: Lawrence Luser
Artists: Phil Kirchmeier
Glenda Oslage

Cover photo by Chris Becker and Darla Gawelski

R. T. Walter

1. Workbench Equipment

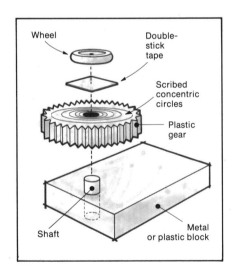

Miniature turntable. Here is a gadget that makes it easy to paint wheels and tires. Purchase a plastic gear from a radio and television parts supply store and slip it on to an axle mounted on a block made from metal or plastic. With a circle template, scribe concentric circles on the tip of the gear to center the wheel. Attach the wheel to the gear with double-backed tape. Turn the gear with your finger as you hold the paintbrush on the wheel. Allow the wheel to dry thoroughly before painting the other side.

Ed Kolbush

Hole cutter. I use a hole saw in a power drill to cut round bulkheads out of sheet plastic to back up radial engines. These come in many sizes, but if you can't find one exactly the right size, make the bulkhead the next larger size and turn it down. Insert a small bolt through the pilot hole in the bulkhead, use double nuts to prevent the plastic from turning on the bolt, and grind it down on sandpaper or a file.

Wayne A. Denny

Keep your files clean. An economical and effective way to keep tiny modeling files clean and free from putty buildup is to use a suede brush. These brushes have brass bristles and do a splendid job on the small files we use so often. They're sold in most variety, drug, and grocery stores, often for less than a dollar.

Dave Musikoff

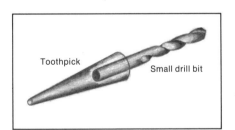

Small drill holders. Cut a round toothpick in half and drill a hole into it with the same drill bit you wish to create a holder for. It's easiest to keep the drill bit stationary in a vise or locking pliers and turn the toothpick onto it. The bore should be about one-third the length of the drill bit. After the bore is made, place a tiny drop of super glue in the bore and insert the butt end of the drill. Colored toothpicks can be used to color code different bits.

Gary Juran

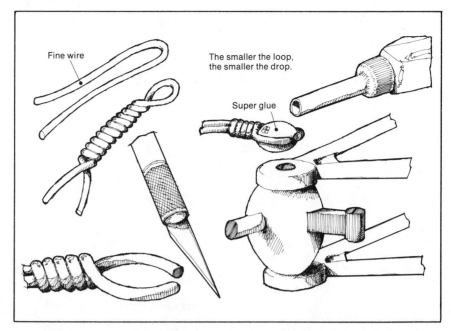

Wire glue applicator. I made this tool to apply single drops of super glue (cyanoacrylate). First, twist a strand of fuse wire (or any fine wire) to form a tiny loop. Next, cut the loop open with a knife. The loop will hold a small drop of super glue. When the drop is touched to the surface you want to glue, it flows out of the loop through the gap.

Giuseppe Bertocchi

Nail buffer. I've found that a chamois nail buffer is well suited to several modeling tasks. It removes scratches from plastic (even clear parts), and it's less messy than a polish. Another application is to give a flat finish a worn, weathered sheen. Light buffing gives a shiny, almost oily appearance to flat paints. This is especially effective on the hoods of armored vehicles, the upper surfaces of aircraft, and even the helmets of figures. Areas around raised details stay flat and thus stand out. This also works well on instrument panels first painted white, then black, and buffed to bring out the raised, white dials.

Dave Orloff

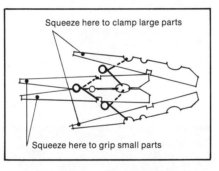

More on clothespins. Here's another way to use spring-type clothespins for clamps. A single clothespin can't grip large assemblies, so I modified two pins and three springs for a multipurpose clamp. The clothespin in the center grips small assemblies, and the outer set handles big jobs.

Shmuel Klahr

Sanding tool. Cut a few pieces of thick plastic ½" x 2½". The plastic should be thick enough to bend without kinking. Next, cut strips of sandpaper ½" x 5½" and form them into loops with the abrasive side out and with a ¾" overlap. Staple the strip through the overlap and bend the plastic strip to fit inside the loop, creating a bow. Move the stapled joint from one end of the plastic bow to the other to expose fresh abrasive.

Ed Kolbush

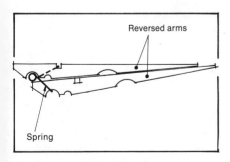

Clothespin clamp. Many modelers use clothespins to clamp parts while the glue sets. Here's a modification of the standard spring-type clothespin. To prevent it from slipping off tapered surfaces like wings, glue thin strips of foam rubber to the clamping sides.

Don Frankfort

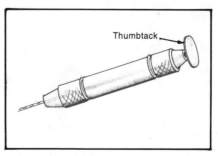

Comfortable pin vise. A double-ended pin vise is easier to use if you put a thumbtack in the unused end. Don't chuck it tight; instead, let it swivel. Now you won't wear a blister in the palm of your hand!

Thomas Herrmann

Double cutters. Make a homemade "cheat line" cutter by super gluing two knife blades together and squeezing them into the handle. Another cutter can be made by bolting two razor blades together. Insert washers between the blades to adjust the width of the cut. Use these cutters to scribe straight or curved lines out of solid-color decal sheet or frisket film.

Burr Angle and Paul Boyer

3

Two-in-one tool. Removing a joint line inside the intake of aircraft like the A-7 and F-8 can be tough. I have devised a tool that works and can be made in minutes. You'll need a Popsicle stick, a plastic-foam egg carton, and wet/dry sandpaper.

Square and taper the rounded end of the Popsicle stick and use it as a putty spreader. Apply putty to the seam, then insert the spreader as far back as possible and smooth out the soft putty.

Super glue a 1″-long piece of plastic foam to the other end of the stick. Cut sandpaper to fit, and glue it to the foam to make a sanding stick.

The foam pad allows the sandpaper to conform to the shape of the intake. You now have a tool that can easily reach inside those tricky areas and smooth the putty.

Rusty White

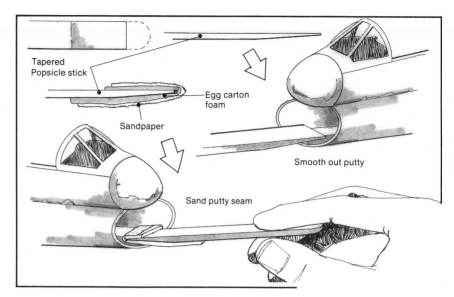

Tapered Popsicle stick
Egg carton foam
Sandpaper
Smooth out putty
Sand putty seam

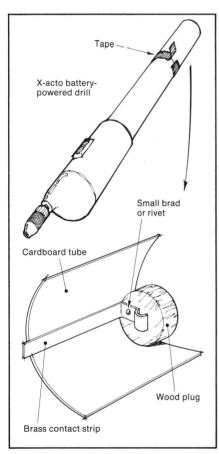

Tape
X-acto battery-powered drill
Small brad or rivet
Cardboard tube
Wood plug
Brass contact strip

Souped-up drill. When I need more power from my motor tool, I use this special setup to hold another battery. It won't harm the motor, but should only be used when you need extra speed or power. Make a ½″-diameter, ¼″-thick wood plug and tack a ¼″ x 3″ brass contact strip to it. Glue the plug to the long edge of a piece of cardboard 2½″ wide and 4½″ long. When the glue dries, roll the cardboard around the plug and glue it all the way around. Make sure the brass strip makes contact with its counterpart in the drill, then tape the cardboard tube to the drill.

Frank Kappel

Cheap knife. I found a bargain at K mart — a package of two hobby knives for $1. Each knife has 12 razor-sharp, snap-off blades. Each package contains one small and one large knife. I like my X-ACTO, but I love my K mart knives.

Denzil Coppler

Model manicure. Emery boards are small fingernail finishing tools that have coarse grit on one side and fine grit on the other. They cost as little as 15 cents each and are ideal for sanding putty and seams. Look for them in drugstores.

Jay Curtin

Plastic bottle containers. Bottles for contact lens solution make good containers for thinner. Pry the caps off and let them dry for a few days, then fill them with thinner. To avoid accidents, clearly label the contents. Make sure the thinner won't affect the plastic.

Paul Boyer

Workbench surface. Secure a ⅛″ sheet of Plexiglas to the top of your workbench (I use a piece of glass about 12″ x 16″). It's an easy-to-clean cutting surface. A white sheet of paper under the glass provides a good contrast with most parts. Put a thin ruler under the glass and it's always where you can use it.

John Staehle

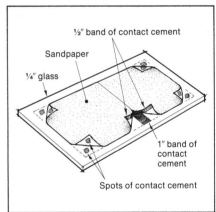

½″ band of contact cement
Sandpaper
¼″ glass
1″ band of contact cement
Spots of contact cement

Large sanding surface. Building a large vacuum-formed kit requires a large, flat sanding surface to remove extra plastic from fuselage and wing halves. Instead of taping or pinning sheets of sandpaper to a board, check with a glass supplier for salvaged plate glass ¼″ or thicker. You can have glass cut to your specifications to fit your workbench exactly.

Attach sheets of sandpaper to the glass using contact cement. Contact cement sets quickly, it's waterproof, and it won't slip. Place a drop of cement about ½″ from each corner, press it down on the glass to transfer some of the cement, and lift off quickly. After the cement dries, reposition the paper and press firmly.

When butting sheets of sandpaper together, smooth a band of cement 1″ wide on the glass and ½″ bands on the back edges of the sandpaper. Avoid getting cement on the grit side of the sandpaper. When the cement bands are dry, smooth the edge of one sheet down on the glass and butt the second sheet as tightly as possible. Attach the other corners as before.

Fred Helmick

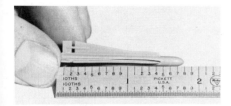

Decimal ruler. Have you ever used an electronic calculator to figure a scale problem and it gives you an answer like 3.77 inches? How much is .77 of an inch? You can either employ complex conversion formulas or you can purchase a ruler graduated in tenths and hundredths of an inch. General Hardware makes a 12″ model (No. 1216) which also features 32nds and 64ths on the other side. Pickett makes two 6″ models (Nos. 419M and 33E).

Paul Boyer

Plastic foam. Plastic foam packaging material can be used to hold paint jars, cement bottles, and airbrushes. Cut the holes you need with a sharp knife or a PVC tube.

Brian Kawczynski

Flexible guide. I use a draftsman's erasing shield as a guide when scribing panel lines on model aircraft. It's flexible enough to follow contours. Some of the small templates in the shield may match doors and access panels.

Lee Coll

Clip-on sanding disks. The Merit clip-on sanding attachment has become the most valuable single tool I own. Although the disks come in a variety of sizes, I find that the 1½″-diameter disk is best suited for hobby work. The ⅛″ shank fits a standard motor tool. Its greatest feature is that the sanding disks snap on and off easily, allowing you to switch from coarse to medium or fine grit in seconds. It gets into spots larger disks can't, and there is no center mounting screw to get in the way of the work. I've used it with great success on all materials — white metal, brass, epoxy, wood, and plastic. The coarse grit is excellent for removing lots of material quickly; it's the only hand tool I've found that is powerful enough to do this job well on metal figures. An adjustable speed control is helpful, particularly when you're working with plastic that melts at high speeds. Look for Merit abrasives at hardware stores.

Shep Paine

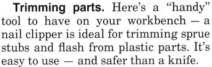

Trimming parts. Here's a "handy" tool to have on your workbench — a nail clipper is ideal for trimming sprue stubs and flash from plastic parts. It's easy to use — and safer than a knife.

Albert Lui

Handy tool. Small manicure scissors are valuable for cutting and boring plastic models. You can remove parts from sprues or use the scissors to replicate battle damage.

Gregory Weeks

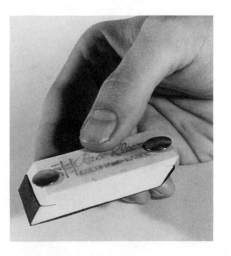

Miniature sander. Make a sanding block using a rubber eraser (look for school supplies). Simply cut a slot at each end, insert a strip of sandpaper, and anchor it with thumbtacks. The eraser is firm yet flexible, just right for delicate sanding jobs.

Ed Kolbush

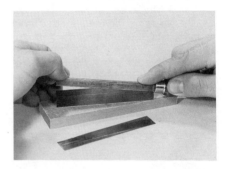

Reversed blades. Razor saw blades are usually installed so that the blade cuts on the push stroke. If you would feel more at ease with a blade that cuts on the pull stroke (as do many other handsaws), simply pry the blade from the U-shaped metal channel that serves as the blade holder, and reverse the blade. Mark the handle with colored tape so you can distinguish this saw from others.

Burr Angle

Food bags. To keep auto body putty from drying in the tube, store it in a resealable plastic bag. They're a lot cheaper than buying a new tube of putty. They are also ideal for storing decal sheets.

Dave Musikoff

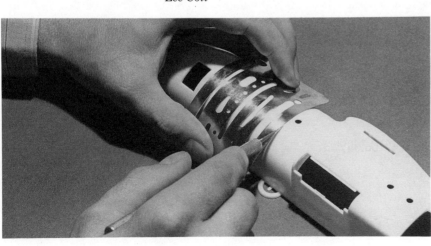

Cushion grips. It's annoying to work with round-handled tools that constantly roll off your workbench, and with knives it's downright dangerous. Here's a solution to the problem: Go to a stationery store and buy several Grip-Rite Cushion Grips. These are 1½"-long triangular pieces of soft plastic with a hole in the center. They're supposed to be finger cushions on pencils, but I cut each of them into shorter sections and slide the sections onto round handles. They keep tools from rolling. The grips come in several colors, so you can color code tools. [See *Sources*, page 48.]

Burr Angle

Waterline marker. Use a "helping hands" or "third hand" holder to help you mark the waterlines on ship models. Disassemble the main sliding arm: Its mounting hole is the perfect size for a pencil or drafting pen. The holder will keep the marker at the same level as you mark the hull. [See "Helping hands," *Sources*, page 48.]

Paul Doman

Resin applicator. When mixing casting resins, the pros use an expensive bell jar with a vacuum system to draw air bubbles from the mix. Here's a cheaper alternative that you can use at home: Pour the mixed resin in a food storage plastic bag, seal it, and squeeze and knead the bubbles to the surface. Once the resin is clear, hold the zipper end up, cut a bottom corner off, and squeeze the resin into the mold.

Ray Anderson

WARNING: Shocks can kill. Don't make 110VAC connections without proper training and tools.

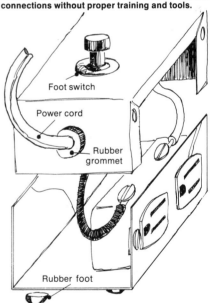

Foot switch
Power cord
Rubber grommet
Rubber foot

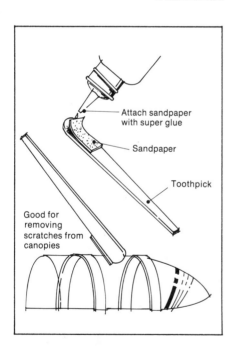

Attach sandpaper with super glue

Sandpaper

Toothpick

Good for removing scratches from canopies

Sanding tool. Trying to sand in small areas with pieces of wet/dry sandpaper torn from a sheet can be clumsy. Instead, cut small strips of sandpaper and attach them to flat or round toothpicks with white glue or super glue. These sanding sticks are particularly useful for sanding scratches out of canopies and removing flash from hard-to-reach areas on figures and landing gear struts.

Mike Chevalier

Convenient trash bag. For those of us who don't enjoy the luxury of a full-time workbench, cleanup at the end of a modeling session can be a chore. To make it a little easier, tape the long side of a large grocery bag on the edge of your workbench. It's easy to drop trash into it without fouling the floor or rug with litter. When you're finished working, just sweep any additional trash over the edge of the table and into the bag.

Jack Clark

Drill bit extenders. Here's a way to drill small holes in tight spots or where an irregular surface won't allow a drill chuck or pin vise to get close. Make an extension by super gluing the drill bit into tubing that has an inner diameter close to the drill size.

Alan Ernat

Foot switch. Here's a tip for any modeler who has ever wished he had more than two hands: Make a foot switch for your motor tool or compressor. I bought the metal chassis box (part No. 270-23) and the pushbutton on/off switch (part No. 275-8051, 6-amp contacts) from Radio Shack. Cut holes in the chassis box for the switch and the electrical outlet. Assemble the box with sheet-metal screws, and attach self-adhesive rubber feet to the bottom of the box. *Caution!* Don't attempt to build this switch unless you are familiar with proper methods for making 110VAC connections.

Felix Leung

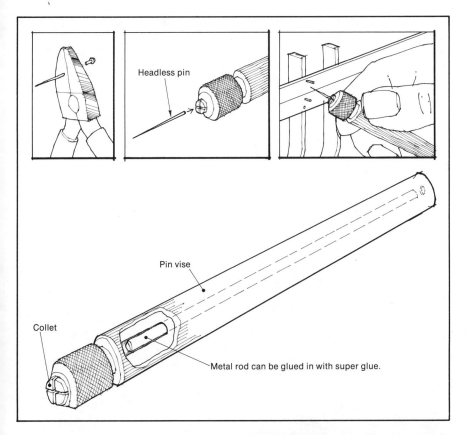

Pin vise

Collet

Metal rod can be glued in with super glue.

Headless pin

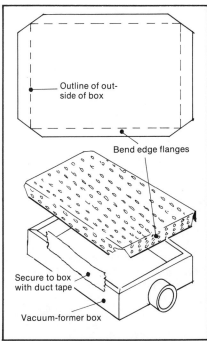

Outline of out-side of box

Bend edge flanges

Secure to box with duct tape

Vacuum-former box

Pin pusher. I build plank-on-frame model ships. After wearing holes in my fingertips pushing pins into wood, I devised my own pin pusher. I took a standard pin vise and inserted a metal rod inside the body. After cutting the heads off the pins, I insert them in the vise, set the collet so that it holds the pins loosely, and use the tool to push the pins into the model. Cut off the excess with a flush-tip cutter.

Norman Emslie

Sticky clay. How often have you wished for three, four, or five hands? Or wished you had a better tool than that super catapult, the tweezer, for picking up and holding small parts? The perfect answer is a British product called Bostik Blu-Tack, manufactured in the U. S. by Black and Decker, and marketed by Bostik, Middleton, Massachusetts. [See *Sources*, page 48.] It looks like modeling clay but acts as a clean working glue.

I find many uses for it: I use it to hold parts together during conversions; I put a slab of it under my bottle of liquid glue so I won't knock it over; I roll it into thin strips to pick up small parts; and I use it to attach figures to my painting stand.

Dick Hirdes

Vacuum-former part. When I made a vacuum former, I used perforated aluminum for the top plate. You can find perforated aluminum at hardware stores and lumberyards, usually in a 3′ x 3′ sheet, which is more than enough. Use duct tape to secure the aluminum sheet to the top of the box. It sure beats drilling all those holes!

Steve Smith

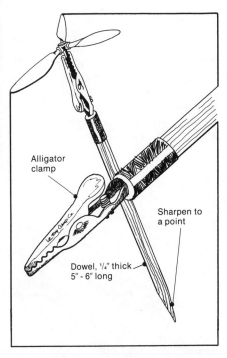

Alligator clamp

Sharpen to a point

Dowel, 1/4″ thick 5″ - 6″ long

Turntable. If you need a small turntable as a paint stand or display base, simply buy one of the plastic versions made by Rubbermaid. If you need something sturdier, make the table from plywood or composition board and mount it on lazy Susan bearings marketed by En-Pak. [See *Sources*, page 48.] The bearings are available in hardware and home-improvement stores in several sizes: 3″ (about $1.99); 4″ ($2.49); 6″ ($3.99); and 12″ ($8.99).

Burr Angle

Parts holder. I make small parts holders out of alligator clips and a 1/4″ dowel. Push the clip on one end and sharpen the other so you can stick it in a block of foam. Several styles of alligator clips are available from Radio Shack; a pack of 10 costs $1.50-$2.50 (depending on the style).

Fred Amos

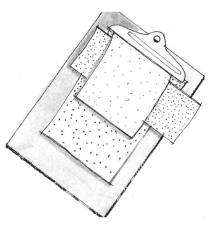

Storing sandpaper. I use a common clipboard to hold sheets of sandpaper. They come in various sizes and can be hung on the wall near your workbench. Most stationery and bookstores carry clipboards.

Vincent Stokes

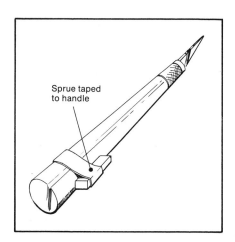

Safety tip. When a hobby knife falls to the floor (or on your foot), it tends to land point first. Tape a small piece of sprue to the handle — no more rolling knives!

Gary Wilson

Padded tweezers. If you have to handle a delicate small part, wrap a small piece of masking tape around the ends of your tweezers to keep the metal from marring the surface.

Mark Savage

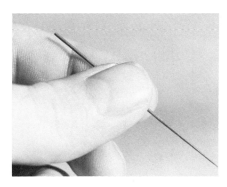

Micro-files. Woodcraft micro-needle files are ideal for boring out gun barrels, cleaning up engraved control-surface hinge lines, and many other delicate jobs. A set of 12 costs $9.95, and includes files in a variety of shapes. The files are 4″ long with a 1/16″ shank. [See *Sources*, page 48.]

Bruce Beamish

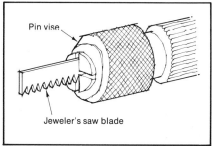

Mini-saw. Break a jeweler's saw blade into sections and insert them in a pin vise. They're great for cutting in tight places. Don't use a lot of pressure, though, because they break easily; it's a good idea to wear safety goggles.

Paul Hicks

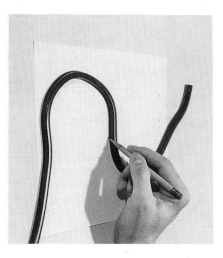

Flexible curve. Draftsmen and artists use a flexible curve — a long, thin bar of soft metal encased in flexible plastic — to transfer shapes or patterns from drawings to working material. It works great on scale plans and for drawing patterns on sheet styrene or wood. Look for it at art supply stores or college bookstores.

Mark Savage

Inexpensive magnifiers. Drugstore variety reading glasses (or diopters) can help modelers in painting and detailing tiny objects. These glasses allow your eyes to focus more comfortably on close work. What's more, they are inexpensive!

Rick and Janine Bennett

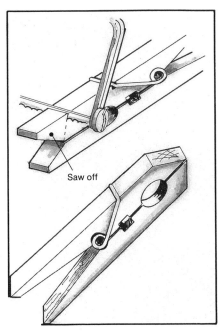

Parts holder. After buying my first airbrush, I had problems holding small parts while painting them. Locking tweezers are one answer, but they're expensive.

I decided to modify clothespins instead. I started with one that had flat surfaces, then I cut the jaws to bring the tip to a flat point. This way small parts can easily be held for painting.

David E. Ligman

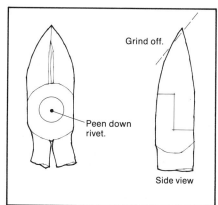

Flush-tip cutter. If you grind down the tip of a standard pair of diagonal side cutters, they can cut parts from sprues flush to the surface of the part. I also advise peening the rivet to keep the tool tight with no side play. As you grind the tip, dunk the tool occasionally in cold water to maintain the temper of the steel.

Frank Kappel

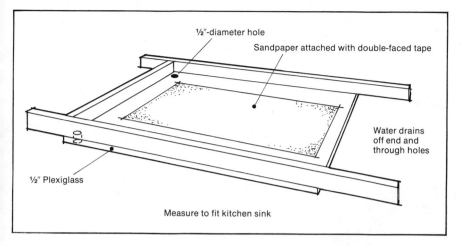

½"-diameter hole

Sandpaper attached with double-faced tape

Water drains off end and through holes

½" Plexiglass

Measure to fit kitchen sink

Sanding board. Wet sanding excess plastic from vacuum-formed parts can be messy, so I made a sanding board from scrap ½" Plexiglas that fits into my kitchen sink. It has two side rails to support the board beneath the faucet. The bottom piece is shorter than the sink so the water can run off. Two ½"-diameter holes also aid drainage. The wet/dry sandpaper is held in place with several full-length strips of double-backed tape. Wet sanding is easier because it keeps the sandpaper from clogging with dust.

Mike West

Another air source. Most inexpensive (about $100) compressors are noisy and the air pressure can't be regulated. Here's a solution. Purchase a Midwest Products air tank for about $36 (available in the automotive department of most K marts); a Sears air line regulator (catalog reference: Division 9, part No. 16042), about $10; two ¼" male fittings and Teflon tape, about $4; and a low-cost air compressor. I bought a compressor designed to plug into a car's cigarette lighter, available at most department and auto stores for about $20. I also recommend an air hose with a built-in moisture trap.

You now have regulated air for about $70. You'll have noiseless operation, no air loss (use Teflon tape for all fittings), portability, and plenty of air for one or more projects.

Caution! Don't exceed the rated capacity of either the air tank or your airbrush and hose. A regulated air line pressure of 15-20 pounds is plenty for most modeling work. *Keith Koenig*

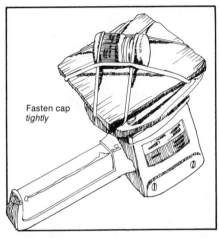

Fasten cap *tightly*

Paint shaker. You can turn a sander into a paint shaker. Hook two heavy rubber bands diagonally across the face of the sander's pad. Drop one or two beebees in the bottle of paint, then put the bottle under the *bottom* bands where they cross in the middle (the bands crossing over provide added tension). Turn the sander on for 15-20 seconds; your paint is mixed! Make sure the bottle cap is tight or you might make a colorful mess. Protect the sander's pad by putting a piece of cardboard over the pad before attaching the bottle of paint.

Steve Flatt

Spare parts organizer. If you have a big collection of spare parts rattling around in a couple of large boxes, use workbench organizers to keep them sorted. You can find them at hardware or discount stores.

Carter Stanley

Handy holder. A draftsman's lead holder holds propellers, landing gear struts, control sticks, and other small parts for painting. A push on the end of the shaft releases the chuck, which can hold a rod up to ³/₁₆" in diameter.

John Merz

Bit cleaner. To clean styrene dust out of your files and motor tool grinding bits, soak them in liquid cement, paint remover, or lacquer thinner for a few hours.

John Downey

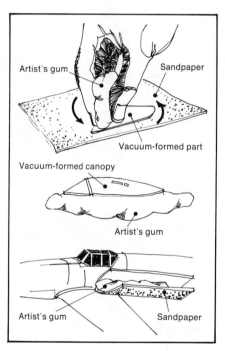

Artist's gum

Sandpaper

Vacuum-formed part

Vacuum-formed canopy

Artist's gum

Artist's gum

Sandpaper

Artist's gum. There are many uses for artist's gum or temporary tacking putty like Eberhard Faber's "Hold It." I use it to grip vacuum-formed parts while sanding the edges: The gum holds as firmly as masking tape but won't come off when wet sanding. I also use it to support vacuum-formed canopies while I mask and paint. A small, sausage-shaped piece of gum wrapped in sandpaper allows me to sand difficult areas like wing/fuselage joints. It conforms to the surface, but it gives enough support to the sandpaper to get the job done.

Lee P. Coll

9

Sanding tool. When sanding seams near landing gear bays, I wrap sandpaper around a small piece of Plastruct I beam and hold it in place with angled tweezers.

Brian Kawczynski

Sanding pads. A useful sanding tool is a circular sanding pad found in hobby shops or the beauty-products section of drugstores. It has sanding paper glued to a plastic-foam core. Like an emery board, it has coarse grit on one side, fine on the other. Only the black ones have waterproof adhesive, so beware. *L. "Willy" Williams*

Painting stand. Here's a way to paint all sides of a model without cumbersome dowels, handles, or bent wire. I use a double-decker plastic "lazy Susan" (a single-level lazy Susan will work, but not as conveniently). The top is the painting level, while the bottom level is used to keep your paint or thinner out of the way but close at hand.

Cut a piece of thick acetate to fit the plate and hold it in place with double-backed tape. This provides a smooth, flat surface to lay the model on. Simply place the model on the plate and rotate the plate to paint the model. The plate is large enough to hold most 1/72 or 1/48 scale models; for larger models, add a piece of Masonite or plywood on top of the lazy Susan.

Phil Kirchmeier

beeswax lasts for years. Buy it at any fabric store or art supply store.

Burr Angle

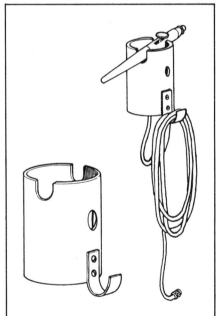

Hold it right there. After ripping my airbrush out of its flimsy metal holder for the umpteenth time, I designed my own device. It won't keep you from getting your feet tangled with the air line, but you'll never yank your airbrush onto the basement floor again. All you need is a 5"-long section of 2" PVC pipe.

File a rest for the airbrush on one end of the pipe. Drill a 1/2" hole in one side of the pipe (to allow screwdriver access), and a 1/8" hole on the opposite side of the pipe (for a mounting screw). Bend a 4"-long strip of 1/16" brass into a "J" shape. Mount this strip below the 1/2" hole, then attach the pipe to the side of your workbench.

When you're not using the airbrush, coil the air line and hang it up!

D. Mulligan

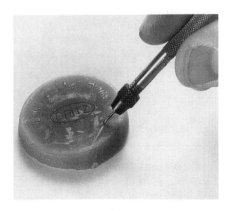

Beeswax. In the old days, I lubricated saw blades and drills with Vaseline when working with styrene and Plexiglas. This kept the blades and drills from sticking to the work and increased the life of the tool. The only difficulty was that Vaseline left a greasy residue. One day a friend suggested beeswax as a lubricant for blades and drills. It works great! It's easier to use and because less is required, cleaning up is not as big a chore. A small cake of

Magnifying table. I made my own magnifying table using an inexpensive plastic magnifying sheet (available from mail-order gift shops). Cut a wood frame to fit the plastic sheet, add pine support strips on the edge of the frame, and make legs from plywood. I used 2" carriage bolts to make the magnifying table adjustable.

C. M. Christoff

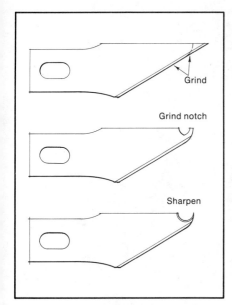

Homemade scriber. It is easy to make a styrene scriber from old, dull No. 11 hobby-knife blades. First, grind down the cutting edge and tip. Next, grind a small notch in the top of the blade and sharpen the whole edge. The blade can be resharpened by repeated grinding.

Seth L. Jones

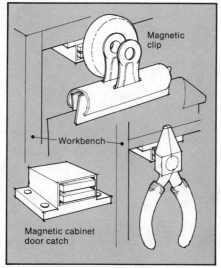

Magnets. A neat and orderly work area is a great help in producing quality models. One way to help keep everything in its place is to use magnetic cabinet door catches as tool holders. They can also be combined with magnet-backed paper clamps to hold plans, reference material, and so forth. Hardware stores and home centers stock good selections.

Jack Clark

Manicure kit. So you got a manicure kit last Christmas and you're thinking about giving it to someone else next Christmas? Take another look — it's a modeler's tool kit! The toenail clippers cut parts from sprues, cuticle scrapers are putty spatulas, and you can always use the nail file, tweezers, and scissors.

Paul Boyer

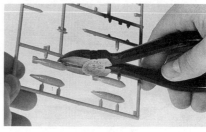

Diagonal cutters. Use diagonal-cutting pliers to chop plastic parts from sprues. They cut neatly and are safer than a knife.

Paul Boyer

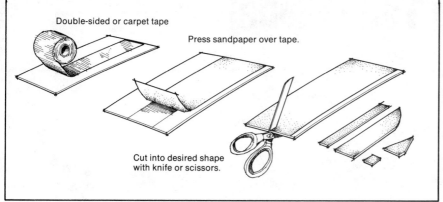

Miniature C-clamps. Ever see those little plastic key ring holders with the spring-loaded clips at the check-out counters? They make excellent C-clamps for holding small parts while glue sets. They're inexpensive, usually less than a dollar.

Steven Smith

Sanding blocks. Here's a way to make sanding blocks to suit nearly every sanding situation. First, cut the top from a plastic-foam egg carton and apply double-backed tape or carpet tape to one side. Next, lay sandpaper over the tape and press firmly. Cut out the size and shape sanding block you need with a knife or scissors. Carpet tape holds the sandpaper, even during wet sanding.

Paul Hicks

Gerry Humbert

2. Assembling Your Model

Photocopying plans. Most copiers are limited to 60 percent reduction, 141 percent enlargement. If your plans fall outside this range, here is a way to figure out the copier setting and number of generations required to obtain drawings in the scale desired. You'll need a calculator or logarithm tables.

The first step in converting 1/96 scale drawings to 1/48 scale is to divide 96 by 48: $96 \div 48 = 2.00$; enlarge the drawing 200 percent. Find the square root of 2. It's 1.4142, or, rounded off, 1.41, which can also be expressed as 141 percent. Copy the original at 141 percent, copy *that* at 141 percent, and the drawing will be the right size $(141 \times 141, \text{ or } 141^2)$.

Some conversions require three generations. Use the cube root to determine the size at which to make copies. For example, to convert 1/96 scale to 1/53 scale: Divide 96 by 35 (2.7428), then find the square root of 2.7428. It's 1.66, or 166 percent, still outside the range of the copier. But calculate the *cube* root of 2.7428: The answer is 1.4007; rounded off, 1.4. To get the right size, copy the original, then the copy, then *that* copy, all at 140 percent.

To make sure that the photocopier is accurate, check a 100 percent copy with a ruler.

Steven Smith

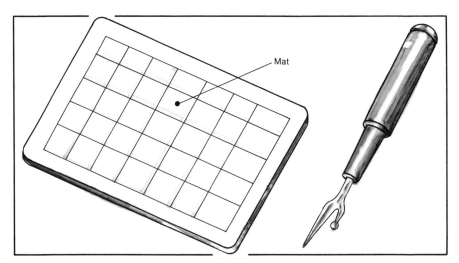

Mat

Cutting suggestions. Special cutting mats, available from art supply stores, provide a nonskid surface and increase the life of blade tips.

The perfect tool for making clean, sharp creases is a seam ripper. The tip is sharp enough for a good score line, but it won't cut through paper. These tips are intended for builders of paper models, but they may help other modelers, too.

Corbin Haldane

Coming unglued. You can remove tube-glue plastic cement by dipping the bonded parts in paint thinner (mineral spirits) or brushing the thinner on the parts, letting the thinner dry, then pulling the bonded surfaces apart.

George Guerra

Keeping track of small parts. Double-backed tape stuck to sheets of cardboard can be used to keep small parts together while working on a model. Then you won't lose them in the clutter of your work area or in your spares box.

Paul Adams

Sagging tracks. This tip works well for tanks with small gaps between the track and hull. After gluing, wedge toothpicks between the hull and track.
Dan Widger

Tiny parts tip. Before you trim photo-etched parts from their tree, attach a piece of masking tape to the part. That way, it won't go flying into oblivion.
David R. Cornwell

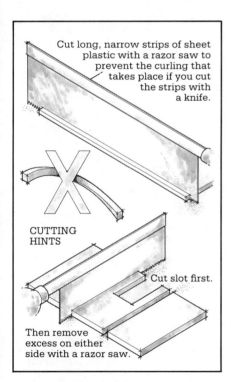

Cut long, narrow strips of sheet plastic with a razor saw to prevent the curling that takes place if you cut the strips with a knife.

CUTTING HINTS

Cut slot first.

Then remove excess on either side with a razor saw.

Cutting hints. To cut small pieces from sheet plastic, use a razor saw instead of a knife when the parts are long and narrow. Cutting thin, narrow strips with a hobby knife usually induces a noticeable curl which is hard to remove. In cutting out a part with a slot in the middle, cut and trim the slots first, then mark the width on each side of the slot. Cut horizontally with a razor saw so the cut is made all at once.
Bruce Culver

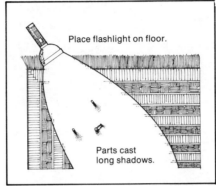

Place flashlight on floor.

Parts cast long shadows.

Part search. Dropped a tiny gray part on a gray floor? You might search forever, but there's an easier way. Place a flashlight on the floor. The elongated shadow cast by the tiny part makes it easy to spot.
Jack Clark

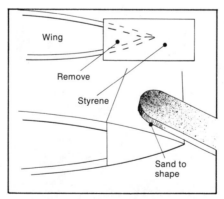

Wing

Remove

Styrene

Sand to shape

Getting the edge. To extend the thin edge of a wing or fin, cut the part back until you reach thicker plastic. It is easier to join the extension to a broad base.
Paul Adams

Hot tip. When using a hot knife in tight spots where adjacent details can be damaged by heat, protect the area with "jigging compound," available at auto-body supply stores.
Barry Lank

Avoid the frost. Ideally, cyanoacrylate (super) glues dry clear. But as with any chemical reaction, many variables can play hob with the results.

I've had the same experience with several different brands of super glues. A technical representative from Pacer Technologies explained the problem to me. The forming of a white deposit is called "chlorosis," caused by the deposit of cured polymer as the cyanoacrylate vapors react with water vapor, the catalyst. In addition, some low-grade polystyrenes enhance this problem with impurities.

You can reduce and perhaps eliminate the problem by ventilating your work area. Use a small fan to blow directly across your workbench. Since the frost is a deposit, light sanding or polishing with rubbing compound or Pacer's Z-7 Debonder can eliminate it.

I don't recommend using cyanoacrylate to attach clear canopies. Frosting can really be a problem when it appears on the *inside* of a canopy that has just been cemented onto a model (no ventilation in there). You can't polish the inside without tearing off the canopy. I've learned my lesson: I attach clear canopies with white glue.
Paul Boyer

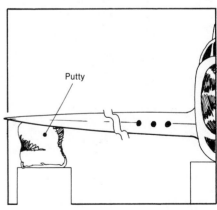

Putty

Silly support. One way to support newly glued parts (aircraft wings, for example) while they dry is with Silly Putty. It's infinitely malleable, does not leave an oily residue, and does not stick to styrene.
Coy London

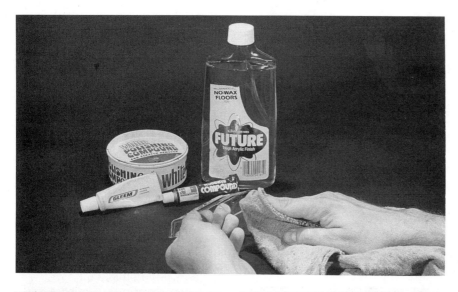

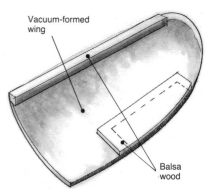

Reinforcements. Glue strip balsa to the halves of vacuum-formed model control surfaces at hinge lines. This provides reinforcement for scribing lines, and allows you to separate and reposition the control surfaces. Lining the leading edges of wings also provides support and a backing for filler.

Bob Lamble

Repairing clear parts. Glue on clear parts is a major problem, and it's not easily cured. In most cases blemishes can be sanded and polished out. First, sand the area with wet 400-grit sandpaper, moving in little circles. It may take a while, but you should be able to smooth out the flaw. Repeat this with wet 600-grit sandpaper, first pressing hard, then gradually easing up on the pressure, again sanding in tiny circles. Then use plastic polish, rubbing compound, or toothpaste (not the gel type)

to polish the area smooth. Keep polishing (it may take a while) until the flaw has disappeared. As a final touch, apply a coat of Future or Brite acrylic floor polish with a soft brush.

In extreme cases, it may not be possible to eliminate the blemish this way. You may have to make a new canopy by vacuum forming over the original. Check with your local modeling club and see if someone who has a vacuum-former might make a copy for you.

Paul Boyer

Model rest. When you're filling, filing, or sanding a seam, or doing other work which requires the model to be held firmly, the only tool that seems to fit the bill is your hands — but you need both to do the work! Fill three-quarters of a plastic sandwich bag with sand or sawdust, remove most of the air, and seal it. Sew a soft cloth bag to cover the plastic, and you have a handy platform to rest your model while you work on it. The sandbag is ideal because it conforms to any contour.

Merle E. Good

Stiff sandpaper. To give sandpaper extra strength and rigidity, apply filament tape to the back. The tape gives it the same strength as emery cloth but allows a greater selection of grit.

H. Homuth

Scribing tool. You can make a scribing tool from a broken drill bit, a file, or a small screwdriver bit. Grind a chisel point on the tool and keep it sharp. The trouble with the knife blade is that it really doesn't remove plastic, it just pushes it aside, creating a ridge on either side of the cut. The scriber, on the other hand, removes the plastic in a long, curly chip (or swarf) in one or two passes. Use a straightedge to keep the panel lines straight. If the tool doesn't cut cleanly, sharpen it.

Paul Boyer

Filling mold marks. Ejector-pin mold marks are difficult to fill, but here's an easy way if you have a Waldron punch set. [See *Sources*, page 48.] I use it to cut out small circles of thin sheet styrene. I then glue the disks into the pin marks. After they're dry I sand them flush. Another way is to cut wafers from sprue (or stretched sprue for smaller circles).

Alan M. Ernat

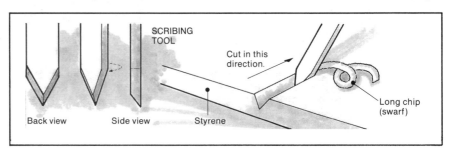

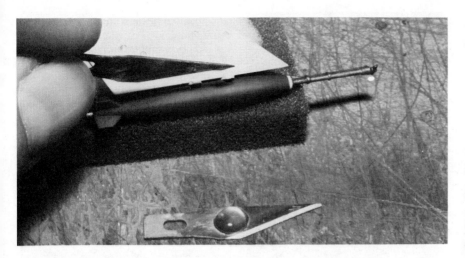

Recycled blades. Here's another use for recycled knife blades — use them as a palette for super glues. Place a drop of super glue on the side of a blade and transfer tiny amounts of adhesive with a pin, wire, or knife blade edge to the parts being assembled. This allows more precise application of glue than the original containers.

Alan Ernat

Helicopter blades. A friend showed me a way to get a realistic sag on model helicopter blades. He strings a wire through the end holes of a hacksaw blade to achieve the required curve (it looks like an archer's bow). Then he tapes a helicopter blade to the hacksaw blade, dips it in hot water for a few moments, removes it, and lets it cool. The plastic blade stays curved.

Paul Squires

Loss prevention. Put sprue trees containing small parts inside a plastic sandwich or food storage bag and cut through the bag to remove the parts from the sprue. The bag allows you to see the parts being trimmed but prevents the pieces from flying across the room and hiding in the carpet.

If you must work in a room with shag carpeting, spread newspaper over the carpet so that you'll at least have a chance of finding dropped parts.

Bruce Culver

Tailored nose weights. Weighting the nose of an aircraft equipped with tricycle landing gear can be tricky. Here's how to make weights that fit exactly to the shape of any aircraft. Fold a 4″ x 8″ piece of aluminum foil in half. Push the foil into the nose of the craft with the eraser end of a pencil. Carefully remove the foil: Now you have a mold in the shape of the aircraft nose. Prop the mold on a piece of scrap wood and use a soldering gun to melt solder into the mold. When the solder cools, remove the foil and admire your custom-fitted nose weight!

Robert Zollo

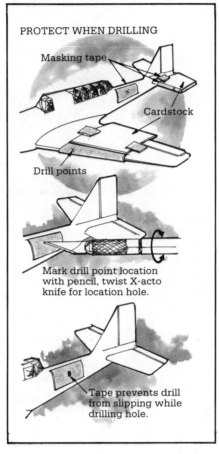

PROTECT WHEN DRILLING

Masking tape

Cardstock

Drill points

Mark drill point location with pencil, twist X-acto knife for location hole.

Tape prevents drill from slipping while drilling hole.

Protect surfaces when drilling. Installing wheels, struts, antennas, machine guns, and similar parts on a nearly completed model, be careful to prevent damage when drilling their mounting holes. Tape thin sections of cardboard (cereal box thickness) to all parts of the model that might be damaged by a slipped drill. Next, apply masking tape directly over the hole locations. Mark the hole locations with a soft lead pencil and then carefully twist the tip of a hobby knife into each mark. Twisting the blade makes a tiny hole in the tape that serves as a drill guide.

Applying the cardboard and tape does take some effort, but I'd rather not spend even more time repairing and repainting damaged sections of the model.

E. Richard Staszak

Quick sanding pad. To sand hard-to-reach areas, wrap a little masking tape onto itself and wrap sandpaper around the wadded masking tape. This makeshift sanding pad is easy to handle; it can be made to any size, and it takes little time to make.

Justin Krauss

Roll sprue over flame

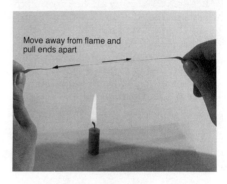

Move away from flame and pull ends apart

Stretching sprue. Light a candle in a safe place (no flammables!) and cut a section of straight sprue 4″ to 6″ long. Hold the middle of the sprue about an inch from the candle flame, and roll the sprue between your fingers so the flame heats it evenly. Continue until the sprue turns glossy and soft, take it away from the flame, and pull the ends apart. The quicker you pull, the thinner the diameter the stretched sprue will be.

Pulling slowly produces thick sections that can be used for boarding ladders and other structural items. A quick, steady pull can give you nearly three feet of thin, constant-diameter stock that's ideal for antenna and rigging wires. If you pull too fast, the sprue will break.

Some styrene stretches better than others, so experiment with different brands. Clear sprue can give the best results if you're looking for ultra-thin stock. Be careful not to ignite the sprue: Styrene fumes aren't good for you, and you'll have little black ashes floating all over the room.

Stretched sprue can be attached with white glue, super glue, or epoxy. I don't recommend liquid or tube plastic cements because they dissolve the thin, fragile plastic.

Paul Boyer

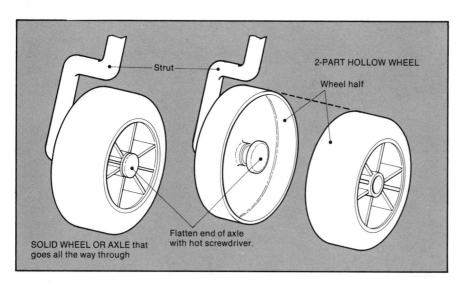

Strut — **2-PART HOLLOW WHEEL**

Wheel half

SOLID WHEEL OR AXLE that goes all the way through

Flatten end of axle with hot screwdriver.

Paul Novak

Reference source. A good reference source for drawings, photos, and histories is the manufacturer of the subject you're modeling. Many corporations respond to requests for information on their products. To find their addresses, check your local library for references such as *Aviation Week and Space Technology, Jane's Weapons Systems, Jane's Fighting Ships,* and *Jane's All the World's Aircraft.*

Rolling along. I don't recommend rolling wheels on aircraft models. The landing gear struts weren't made for that stress; they may break. But if you want them to roll, here's how.

Let's say the aircraft has two-piece wheels. If the axle on the strut doesn't go all the way through the wheel, flatten the end of the axle with the inside half of the wheel mounted. Then reattach the other half of the wheel. If the axle goes all the way through, simply flatten the protruding end.

Paul Boyer

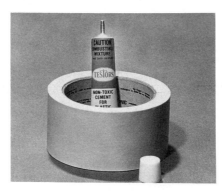

Eliminate the drips. We've all had the contents of a tube of glue or putty ooze out when we forgot to replace the cap. Next time, prop up the tube inside a wide roll of masking or duct tape. This allows repeated use without constant capping and uncapping.

Mark Savage

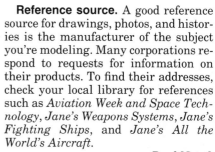

Light source

Wing

Scrape in this direction, working out toward the ribs

Fabric surfaces. Here's a simple method for improving the appearance of fabric-covered ailerons, rudders, and so on. Use a curved-edge hobby knife to scrape away some of the plastic between rib locations. You can create shallow, concave areas which simulate the appearance of tight fabric on full-size aircraft. It helps to shine a strong light across the surface as you're working on it: This lets you see how much you're removing and helps you keep the scraping centered between the ribs.

John Thompson

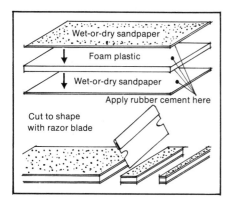

Wet-or-dry sandpaper

Foam plastic

Wet-or-dry sandpaper

Apply rubber cement here

Cut to shape with razor blade

More sanding tips. I make my own sanding blocks by attaching 600-grit wet/dry sandpaper to a sheet of foam plastic. First, cut plastic and sandpaper to the same size, then coat the back of the sandpaper and one side of the foam with rubber cement. Follow the directions for rubber cement — let it dry until tacky, then press the sandpaper to the foam firmly, but not so hard that you crush the foam. Repeat this for the other side. Now you have a sanding block with a flat surface.

This thin sanding block can be cut with razor blades to any shape you need. Cut it with repeated light strokes to avoid crushing the foam. The resulting pieces are like extra-fine files. The narrower the slice, the more fragile it is, but for small areas and delicate sanding it can't be beat. If the foam breaks, cut a new slice.

Michael Phillips

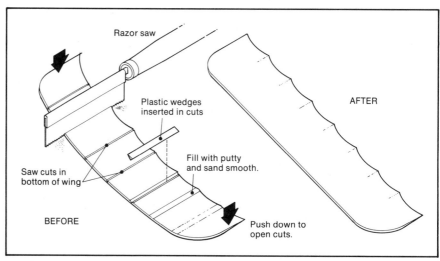

Razor saw

Plastic wedges inserted in cuts

Saw cuts in bottom of wing

Fill with putty and sand smooth.

AFTER

BEFORE

Push down to open cuts.

Straightening wings. Warped wings? The cause of your problem may be too much glue. Split the wing open and reattach with a little liquid cement. If it appears that this would ruin the wing, make several cuts in the underside of the wing and glue in small strips of plastic. These wedges force the wing into the proper shape. I can't predict how many cuts you'll need — just add a few at a time until you overcome the warping. Cover the cuts and strips with filler putty and sand them smooth.

You can immerse the wing in hot water to reshape it. After you get the right shape, tape the wing to a flat surface and let it cool.

E. R. Staszak

Tips for vacuum-form modelers. I used to remove excess material from vacuum-formed parts with a hand-held sanding block and medium- or coarse-grit sandpaper. This was time-consuming and messy.

Now I use a 1″ bastard file to file the flash until it's almost transparent. I hold a sheet of 220-grit wet/dry sandpaper flat against a piece of mirror tile to remove the rest of the excess. This is faster, not quite as messy, and gives me better control.

Detailing cockpits, I've found that dress snaps (sold in fabric stores) make excellent control yokes. The snaps usually require only minor modifications.

Alan C. Griffith

Gentle abrasive. A model has to be free of dirt, grease, and oil so paint will adhere. Soft Scrub, a liquid kitchen cleanser made by Clorox, is a soapy solution containing a mild abrasive that's perfect for cleaning and polishing plastic models before painting. After scrubbing the model, rinse it with warm water and wipe it dry with a lint-free cloth. Soft Scrub also works as a hand cleaner.

Lee P. Coll

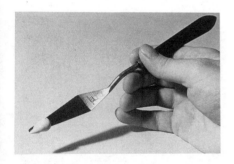

Paint knife. An "artist's spatula" is actually a paint knife which is available in several sizes. This is the smallest one I could find. It's thin and flexible, with a blade that is small enough to apply putty to my 1/72 scale aircraft models.

Will Reynolds

Paper polisher. Wet sanding minor scratches is tedious. Instead, a few seconds of vigorous polishing with a coarse, high-fiber-content paper towel (I use Hi-Dri) does a great job.

Don Frankfort

Old instructions. Don't throw away old kit instructions. They may contain valuable information, and you might need a spare instruction sheet someday. Good instructions have history, painting information, reference numbers, and often several different color schemes.

You can make a copy of the information and file it with your other research data on that subject. Then keep a separate file of old instructions.

Robert Richardson

Children's department. When you go to the library to research a model or diorama, try the children's department. Children's books often have more photos than adults' books.

Leslie Mele

Rigging biplanes. I've always feared rigging biplane models; thread never looked right and I had difficulties using stretched sprue. Now I use monofilament fishing line, available at sporting goods stores. It comes in a variety of thicknesses, rated by strength.

Cut the approximate length of the section needed and attach one end with super glue. After the first end has set, repeat the process at the other end. If there is any sag, tighten it up by passing a burning incense stick near it. The rapid heating and cooling of the line brings it taut.

Matthew McCarthy

Total recall. While researching a model, I often come across information on another subject that I plan to model. As a reminder, I put a card with reference notes — magazine titles, dates — in the kit box. When I get to that project, I won't have to search through my references again.

Blair Yoshida

Soldering surface. When soldering brass parts I tape them in their desired alignment on a piece of ceramic bathroom tile. The tile makes a stable, burnproof work area.

Brian Kawczynski

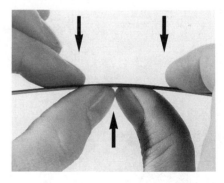

Droopy rotors. I've had good results making model helicopter rotor blades droop by bending them. Don't hold each end and bow it, though: That will lead to instant disaster! Take each rotor blade and apply stress in many areas along its length, starting near the hub end and working outward every half inch or so. I don't bend the outer quarter of the blade.

You can apply too much stress to the blade and break it, so give it just a little bend in each spot. You can always go back and give it more. If you do break a rotor, repair it with liquid glue: I've found that super glues don't have enough strength on a repair with so little surface area. After you have repaired the rotor, you'll have to avoid bending it near the break.

Paul Boyer

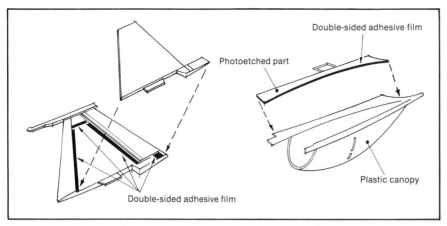

Photoetched part

Double-sided adhesive film

Plastic canopy

Double-sided adhesive film

Attaching photoetched parts. If you have had trouble getting photoetched canopy and cockpit detail sets to lie flush, try using double-sided adhesive film. This translucent film is laminated between two sheets of paper; buy it at an art-supply store. Cut a piece from the sheet, slightly larger than the part you're going to attach. Peel away the backing paper, place the photo-etched part on the film, and trim away the excess by cutting through the second backing sheet. Remove residual film from the cut edges with a rubber cement pickup (also found in art supply stores). Next, remove the second backing sheet and position the part. Gently

press the part down, then place a few drops of super glue along the edge. Capillary attraction carries the glue all along the seam and fills gaps.

I also use double-backed adhesive film for positioning parts. Cut small squares and narrow strips and place them along the bonding surfaces while test fitting. If you need to adjust the fit, simply remove the parts. Once in position, the parts can be welded together with liquid cement — the adhesive film won't inhibit the bond. If the adhesive holds too well, a few drops of paint thinner loosens it. If I need to remove the adhesive, the rubber cement pickup comes to the rescue. *Mark Lewis*

Safety tip. Before you throw out old hobby knife blades, wrap them with tape. Next time you rummage through the trash barrel for the accidentally discarded wheel or decal, you won't cut yourself and introduce family members to strange and unpleasant vocabulary. *Stewart Bailey*

Cement problems. Mix Testor's liquid cement and Testor's tube cement in a 1:1 ratio. The mixture will have the flow of liquid cement and the strength of tube cement with few or no strings. *Dan Prowse*

Wing clamp. I use pliers with plastic-coated handles to squeeze wing halves together while the glue is setting. No, don't use the business end because you'll ruin the surface of the model. Use the *inside* of the handles where the plastic coating can apply gentle pressure without marring the parts. *D. H. Minton*

Heavy irons. Golfer's weight tape (available from most pro shops and used to add more weight to clubs for more striking power) can be cut with scissors and pressed into the nose of a model aircraft to keep it down on the tricycle gear. *Joe Hively*

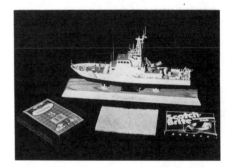

Sanding without sandpaper. I use a kitchen scouring pad (such as Scotch-Brite) for final sanding on all my models. It doesn't leave marks like ordinary sandpaper. *Anthony Kloska*

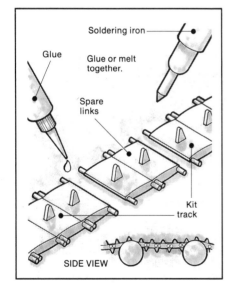

Soldering iron

Glue

Glue or melt together.

Spare links

Kit track

SIDE VIEW

Realistic tank tracks. Tank tracks look more realistic when they drape over the wheels. If your tank kit has extra track, attach it to the end of the main track piece with glue or a soldering iron. The longer track will allow extra slack and the track will sag between each wheel. *Melvin Mays*

Heat source. A small, hand-held hair dryer provides a controllable, and above all, safe source of heat. I use it for working with plastic, but it can also be used to accelerate epoxies. *Dick Hirdes*

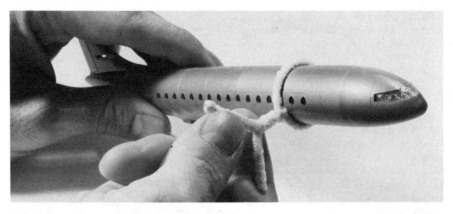

Pipe cleaner vise. Pipe cleaners can be used to hold fuselage halves together while cement sets. Wrap a pipe cleaner around the assembled fuselage and then twist the ends together. They

are stronger than rubber bands and apply even pressure, preventing oval-shaped fuselages that occur when using small vises or C-clamps. *Paul Boyer*

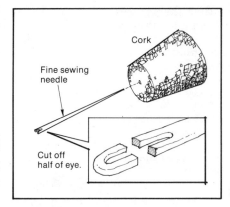

Super glue applicator. Here's my homemade super glue applicator. I cut off the top half of the eye of a fine sewing needle, forming a forked end. The sharp end is put into a cork. Simply dip the open eye into a drop of super glue. A tiny amount of glue will stay in the eye for transfer to your model. The finer the needle, the smaller the drop.

Richard Divald

Aligning with gravity. I had trouble keeping a ship's many stacks, booms, masts, and ventilators truly vertical. I solved the problem by using slow-setting tube cement. Before the glue set, I turned the model upside down in a makeshift jig and allowed gravity to align the parts. Be sure the model is level in each axis while on its back.

Ed Kolbush

Cotton smoke and fire. Years ago I read about a modeler who simulated smoke and fire by painting the fiberglass or polyester strands found in aquarium filters. I tried it but I didn't like the nasty feel of the material.

Now I simply use cotton balls from a first aid kit. I stretch out the cotton and spray it with red and black paint. After these paints dry, I add orange to represent flame.

The cotton smoke and flame can be used to replicate a rocket exhaust, a shell burst, or the flames from burning vehicles and buildings. Unpainted cotton can represent a cannon muzzle blast or even ocean spray.

Edward John Wojcik

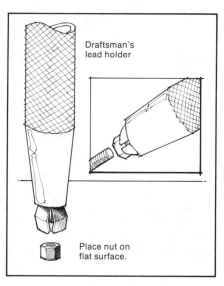

Tiny part holder. A draftsman's lead holder is ideal for holding tiny screws and nuts. Place the nut on a flat surface, put the collet over the nut, and tighten the collet. This makes it easier to thread the nut onto a bolt or screw.

Giuseppe Bertocchi

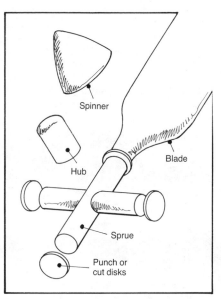

Scratchbuilt props. You can make four-blade props from sprue. Find a four-way intersection on a sprue tree, and cut each "arm" the same length. Glue a small disk on the end of each arm, then glue the blades on the disks. Prop hubs and spinners are optional.

Steven Brooks

Solving the missing link. I ran into a problem with the Kasten German King Tiger tank-tread kit. When I got to the last connection the links did not mate. The solution was simple. Motorcyclists call it a "half link." Ordinarily you would have to skip two pieces of track to mate the links again. A half link eliminates one of those links. It's hard to spot this special link, and by planning ahead you can hide it entirely.

Jack Smith

Disposable palettes. Food jar lids make excellent throwaway palettes for mixing small amounts of paint, holding water for sanding, or holding thinner for cleaning brushes. After they have served their original purpose on their jars, run the lids through a cycle on the upper rack of the dishwasher and they're ready to use.

D. H. Minton

Filling seams. To fill wide and deep seams, glue stretched sprue that is slightly wider than the seam. Press the sprue into the gap and wet it with liquid cement. After the glue sets, sand the sprue flush. *Jack Clark*

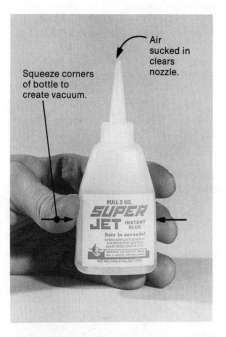

Clog-free super glue bottle. If you use super glue regularly, you know how difficult it is to keep the nozzle clear. I avoid letting the nozzle contact anything. Instead, I squeeze a few drops onto a small tray made from the top of an orange juice can or an upside down paint bottle with a concave bottom. Then I apply super glue with a pin or a toothpick. After dispensing the glue I hold the bottle upright and squeeze the corners, creating a vacuum which draws leftover glue in through the nozzle.

Tommy Thomason

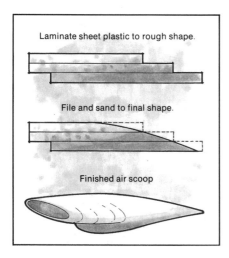

Laminate sheet plastic to rough shape.

File and sand to final shape.

Finished air scoop

Plastic laminate. I have had great success fabricating parts by using laminated sheet plastic bonded with liquid cement. First, I laminate the plastic to the rough shape I need, let the assembly dry for 24 hours, then file and sand to come up with the final shape. I have made cooling scoops, nose cones, and pylons with this method, but just about anything can be produced this way.

Novus H. Henry Jr.

Ounce of prevention. To avoid cutting your fingers and ending up with bandages covering them after carving with your hobby knife, try bandaging your thumb and one or two fingers beforehand. This will eliminate the cuts and relieve some of the apprehension that the blade may slip.

Ed VanTassel

Invisible weight. Although tricycle aircraft can be stabilized by weighting the nose of the aircraft, sometimes there is no invisible place to put the weight. Here's an answer: Make a paste of fine metal filings and epoxy. The paste is surprisingly heavy and can be attached anywhere.

Katherine Michael

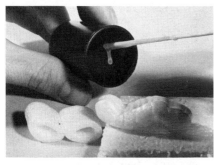

Putty from plastic foam. Here's another home-brew putty. Cut up expanded polystyrene packing material and dissolve it in liquid styrene cement. It dissolves faster than sprue chips and it's easier to cut. It also seems to dry quicker. If it strings, just add more polystyrene.

Dick Hirdes

Baking soda dispenser. Baking soda is often used as a gap filler and accelerator for cyanoacrylate cements; it's inexpensive and sands well. Trouble is, the box spills easily. Here's a tip I found in a Hot Stuff brochure: Buy a 3-ounce ear syringe at a drugstore and cut off the tip to form a hole about 3/16" in diameter. Fill the syringe with baking soda (by suction) and apply the soda by gently tapping the tip on the work.

Burr Angle

Corrugated panels. I make my own 1/35 scale corrugated tin panels with 1 7/16" x 2 3/4" sheets of aluminum foil (the approximate size of a standard sheet of corrugated tin). Use your fingers or an eraser to rub the foil over corrugated tin building material, available from model railroad shops. [See *Sources*, page 48.] You can use the foil panel as is or paint and weather it.

Robert W. Martin

Repairing marred plastic. Cerium oxide, a polishing compound available from a lapidary (gem cutter), works well for removing glue and scratches from clear plastic. First, wet sand with 400-grit sandpaper. Then, wet sand with 600-grit. Finally, rub cerium oxide into the plastic until it becomes shiny. One bag of cerium oxide lasts a lifetime.

Michael Maupin

Hot cutter. It's easier to cut parts from sprues if you heat a blade in a candle flame and press it into the plastic. It should cut cleanly and quickly without deforming the part.

Danny Lin

Easy molds. Mix a small amount of epoxy putty, flatten it to a 1"-thick pancake with a rolling pin, then coat the top surface with a non-stick cooking spray such as Pam. Before the putty cures, press the original part into the putty and lift it back out; make sure the depression has a crisp outline.

When the putty is fully cured, respray with Pam and fill the mold depressions with either a 50/50 mixture of super glue and baking soda (for small parts) or five-minute epoxy (for large parts). I've used this technique to produce inexpensive details.

Barry Lank

Cost-saving materials. Look under "Print and Ink Supplies" in the yellow pages of your phone directory. Silk-screening mesh is available for industrial use in a variety of sizes, both metal and fabric. Fiber metal meshes are good for vent intakes such as those found on the MiG-29. The fabric works well for all types of covering materials. Industrial print suppliers also carry paints, glues, and thinners in economical volumes, along with a wide range of tools.

Bruce Beamish

Easy lathe. I use a 1/4" electric drill as a lathe to manufacture all manner of detail parts, including small tank fittings, gun barrels, even bottles.

Select a round piece of sprue slightly larger than the item to be made and chuck it in the drill. Rotate the drill at high speed and use hand tools — a hobby knife, a file, or sandpaper — to carve and shape the sprue. Pause often to allow the sprue to cool. After achieving the desired shape, hold fine sandpaper against the turning sprue to remove scratches.

Bottles shaped from clear sprue in this manner turn out amazingly clear.

J. T. Coble

Tacky white glue. While helping my wife mount her cross-stitch work I discovered Aleen's Original Tacky Glue. [See *Sources*, page 48.] Its tackiness holds pieces in place as they dry. It's great for installing windshields and canopies because it dries clear and doesn't affect plastic.

Bob Rogers

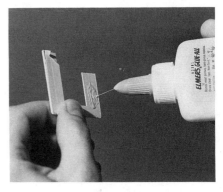

White glue threads. Try thinning the bottle with one or two teaspoonfuls of water. Elmer's Glue-All and similar white glues are based on polyvinyl acetate, a water-soluble compound designed to bond porous surfaces like paper and wood.

Also, try adding a few drops of liquid dishwashing detergent to the bottle of glue and stirring. This acts as a wetting agent, breaking down the surface tension of the glue, which is causing the threading.

Paul Boyer

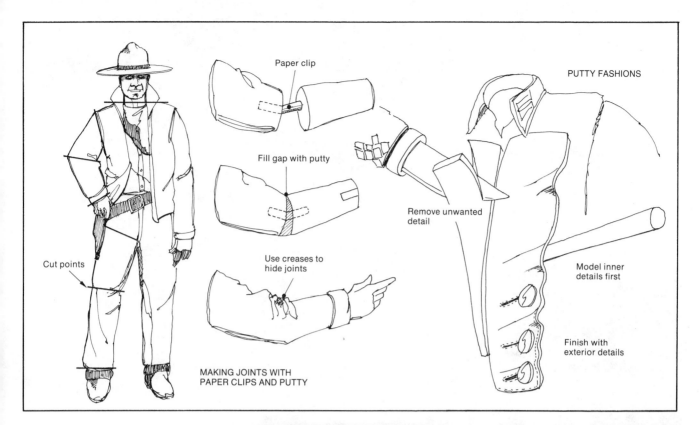

Paper clip

Fill gap with putty

Use creases to hide joints

Cut points

MAKING JOINTS WITH PAPER CLIPS AND PUTTY

PUTTY FASHIONS

Remove unwanted detail

Model inner details first

Finish with exterior details

Modifying figures. You can alter a figure's posture with a paper clip and Duro two-part filler putty (available at hardware stores). Saw through the joint you want to alter. Drill a hole in either side of the joint, and join the parted pieces with paper-clip wire. When you have determined the exact pose you want, super glue the wire. To fill the gap in the joint, roll putty onto the area with a moist toothpick. When you have the shape you want, smooth and blend the joint where the putty meets the figure.

Hilber Graf and Preston Russell

Hand drill

Hole for wire

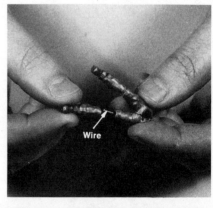

Wire

Putty

Smooth, blend joint

Greg Hildebrandt

3. Masking, Paints, and Decals

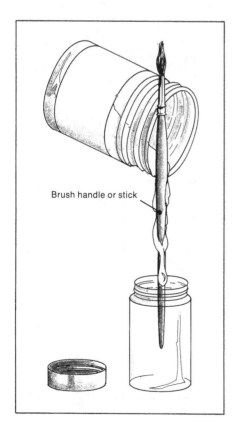

Pouring paint. An oldie but goodie way to pour liquid from one bottle to another is to hold a paintbrush handle over the open top of one bottle as it's poured. Center the handle in the other bottle; this will prevent spilling.

Richard Divald

Brush holder. Use a block of foam plastic or modeling clay to hold brushes upright and out of the way. Simply insert the handle ends into the block.

Chris Morris

Special-effects paintbrushes. Artist's stencil brushes can be used for many modeling tasks. Their short, stiff bristles are useful for dry-brushing and heavy wash applications. Use them to make stippled camouflage patterns and beaded weld seams. They're available in several sizes at art-supply stores.

John Hirschle

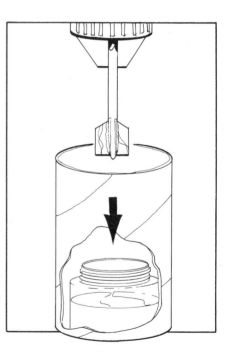

All shook up. Here's how to achieve high-speed paint stirring with no muss, fuss, or expensive equipment.

Cut off the head of a nail and solder a "paddle" of brass sheet on one end of the nail. Chuck the other end of the nail in a variable-speed drill. Before you start to drill, place the cardboard core of a roll of toilet paper over the jar of paint. (By the way, the nail will spin better if you leave a bit of its tip exposed on the "paddle" end.)

Katherine Michael

22

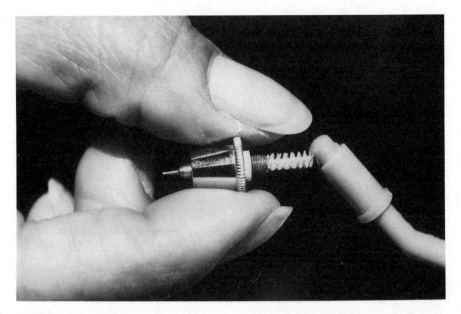

Cleaning airbrushes. The bothersome task of cleaning your airbrush can be made easier. A cylindrical dental brush allows you to reach inside the head and the spray regulator. Dip the brush in cleaning solution and scrub away. Remove paint from the brush with a rag, then repeat the operation until the brush comes clean.

Manuel Ruiz

Spray-on tire tread. I use a piece of plastic window screen as a mask to airbrush tread patterns on my 1/48 scale aircraft tires. First, I spray the tires Floquil Engine Black (R10) and allow them to dry. Next, I cut a ¾"-wide strip diagonally out of plastic window screen. Plastic screen is more flexible than metal, and you can stretch it to form an accurate diamond pattern. I wrap the screen tight around the tire and hold it in place at the bottom with locking tweezers.

Spray the tire with Floquil Grimy Black (R13) to add the tread pattern; only one light coat is needed. Just remove the screen, and you have a realistic worn tread pattern.

Joel Cordsmeyer

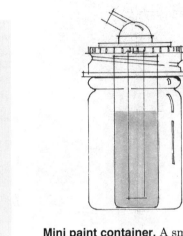

Mini paint container. A small plastic pill vial or other small container can be cut to fit inside the paint jar of your airbrush as a color cup substitute. This setup allows better siphon pickup than you get with a small amount of paint in a larger bottle.

Greg Sacho

Chrome stripper. Don't like that super-shiny chrome on model car parts? You can remove it easily by soaking the parts in vinegar for a few days. This mild acid gradually softens the plating without harming the plastic. A light rub removes the plating.

Ed VanTassel

Foil seals. The thin aluminum foil wrapped around some candy bars makes excellent replacement seals on paint bottles. Clean off the bottle threads and cap, place a piece of foil over the opening, and screw on the cap. The foil keeps the paint from drying out, and the thread and cap clean.

Ed Kolbush

Cheap mask. Instead of expensive, specialized liquid masks, try Elmer's white glue for masking clear surfaces such as windshields and canopies. Apply the glue with a toothpick or a brush. You can peel off the dried glue easily with the tip of a sharp knife.

Jon Dunn

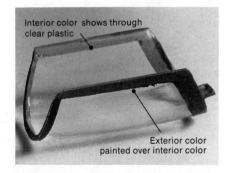

Interior color shows through clear plastic

Exterior color painted over interior color

Cheap primer. Krylon gray (in a spray can) is an efficient and inexpensive primer for big jobs. It's easy to find, doesn't load the sandpaper, and fills small imperfections like "smart" liquid putty. *George Choksy*

Krylon primer. Krylon gray primer, available in a 12-ounce spray can, is a good match for gray FS 36118. To me, gunship gray, NATO and RAF dark sea gray, and Luftwaffe medium gray are all the same as Krylon gray primer. It's easier than hunting for all those other colors! *Michael D. Jones*

Canopy trick. Apply the interior canopy frame color on the exterior first, then cover it with the exterior color. You'll be able to see the interior color inside the canopy.

Paul Boyer

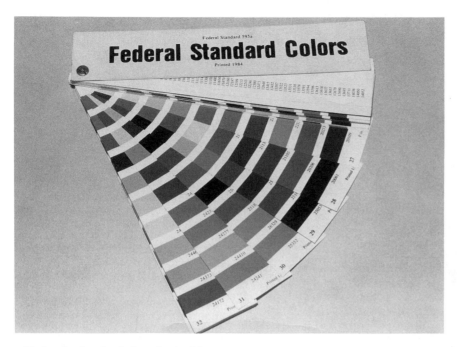

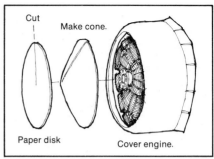
Cut
Make cone.
Paper disk
Cover engine.

Federal standard fan deck. Many kits of modern military aircraft and vehicles include references to Federal Standard 595B colors, and many hobby paint manufacturers mix paints to match these colors. Actual FS595B paint chips on loose-leaf, 3″ x 5″ cards have been available for years. Recently the U. S. government has produced the FS595B in a fan deck, strips of heavy paper held together with a swivel screw.

The beauty of the fan deck is that each 2″ x 5/8″ color chip is printed out to the edge of the strip, making color matching easier — no more folding and bending loose-leaf pages to get the chip close to your sample. The fan deck measures 10″ x 2″ x 5/8″ and fits into your camera bag so you can check the paint on that full-size F-18 at the air show!

The fan deck contains over 500 paint chips and sells for $7.50. The loose-leaf version sells for $9. Make checks or money orders payable to General Services Administration, Specifications Section, Room 6654, 7th and D St. SW, Washington, DC 20407. Enclose a self-addressed, adhesive label.

Paul Boyer

Narrow masking tape. Chartpak or Formaline crepe graphic tape is excellent for masking. It comes in many widths, and in curved lines. Some tape rolls are 600″ long — a lifetime supply. Look for graphic tape in art-supply stores. [See *Sources*, page 48.]

Richard Ziven

Tape remedy. Annoyed by the adhesive residue left on your model by masking tape? Cool it — literally. Put it in the refrigerator for 3-5 minutes. The adhesive fails when it's cold, making it easy to remove.

Katherine Michael

Fine lines. Here is a way to precisely paint circular sections or objects. Select a piece of polyethylene big enough to cover the model (a plastic food bag does the trick). Place a small piece of leather under the middle of the plastic sheet. Make a hole in the middle of the sheet with a 1/4″ leather punch.

For this example, push the nose of the model through the hole. The increasing diameter of the nose section will stretch the opening as you pull the plastic over the nose. When you've reached the end of the area to be painted, check that the plastic is even all around the nose. The rest of the polyethylene protects the model from overspray. Paint the nose, let the paint dry for two or three minutes, then cut with a scissors from the outer edge of the plastic sheet to the middle hole. Then gently unwrap the sheet from the nose. This method works for cowlings, noses, gasoline drop tanks, and other compound curves — adjust the size of the hole to the job at hand.

Manuel Ruiz

Masking radial engines. Here's my technique for masking radial engines inside cowlings. Cut a disk of heavy paper slightly larger than the diameter of the cowl opening. Make one cut from the edge to the center of the disk. By overlapping the paper at the cut, you can make a cone with a base circumference small enough to pop inside the cowl opening. The paper will spring back inside the front lip of the cowl to form a masking shield over the engine. After painting, remove the mask with tweezers.

Bob Rice

Easy mask. Use 3M Post-it notes to mask panel edges. The low adhesion won't mar finished areas, and they're faster and easier to apply and remove than tape.

David Fifer

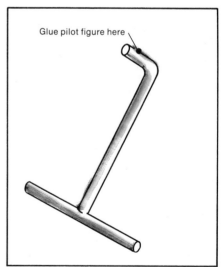
Glue pilot figure here

Painting pilots. Holding pilot figures for 1/72 scale aircraft was frustrating until I learned to glue the pilot to a holder made from sprue. The sprue provides a handle so you can manipulate the figure easily for painting.

You only need two rods of sprue about 2″ long. Make a right-angle bend about 1/2″ from the end of one rod (or use sprue from a corner), then glue the other rod on the straight leg to form a "T." Use tube cement to glue the pilot to the end of the bend (by the seat of his pants). When you're done painting, simply twist him off.

Merle Good

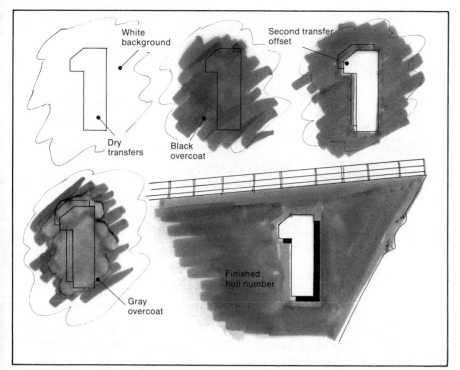

White background

Second transfer offset

Dry transfers

Black overcoat

Gray overcoat

Finished hull number

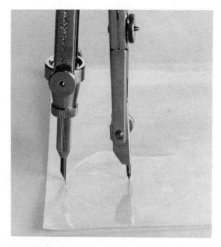

Ship numbers. I use dry transfers as masks for painting drop-shadowed ship numbers. First, paint the area white. After the paint is dry, apply dry-transfer numbers. Now apply a thin coat of black. When that coat is dry, apply an identical set of numbers, slightly offset to the right and down. Overcoat the area with Navy sea gray and let the paint dry for 24 hours to ensure crisp edges on the numbers. Burnish tape over the transfers and peel them off. Remove stubborn bits of transfers with the tip of a hobby knife. The result: a white number with a black shadow on a gray background.   *Rick Lorenz*

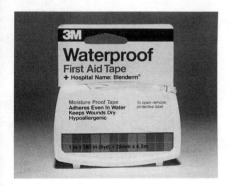

Medical masker. I have discovered 3M Waterproof First Aid Tape (its hospital name is "Blenderm") to be excellent masking tape. It's thin, frosty, has medium-high tack, and is extremely flexible — everything you need in a masking tape. Look for it in drugstores. If you can't find it, ask your pharmacist to order it.

Dr. Robert Bokat

Brush storage jars. It's easy to keep paintbrushes neat and clean when you have a big jar to store them in: Keep an eye on the pepperoni/teriyaki stick/beef jerky jars at your local convenience store. When a jar is down to the last couple of pieces, buy the rest and ask the clerk for the jar. You get a nice plastic jar tall enough to stand your brushes in.

Buck Pilkenton

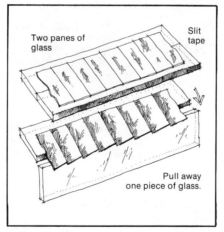

Two panes of glass

Slit tape

Pull away one piece of glass.

Tape handling. Do you find picking up small pieces of masking tape from the cutting surface tedious and annoying? Get a better grip on the problem this way: Butt two pieces of glass together and tape over the seam. Slit the tape into small pieces, cutting across the seam. Then, peel away one piece of glass, exposing one edge of the tape for easy handling.

Ed Kolbush

Brush protectors. The clear plastic tubes that protect fine brushes are easy to lose — drop them on the carpet and the search is on. Paint them a bright color to make them easier to find.

Chris Morris

Masking again. The best way to mask a circle is to use frisket paper (sometimes called frisket film). This is a thin, paper-backed, self-adhesive material used by artists to mask airbrush illustrations. Look for it at art-supply stores.

I use a draftman's compass with a cutting blade in place of the pencil. First, cut the mask for the outside of the circle. Then cut another circle that is 1.5 mm smaller in radius. Discard the inside of the larger circle and the inside of the smaller circle. Apply the frisket outline on the part, then place the smaller circle in the center, making sure that the exposed area is equally thick all around the circle. You'll have to eyeball this, but keep trying.

Once you're satisfied that the frisket is in the proper position, burnish it down with your fingernail. Now you're ready to paint. I recommend airbrushing. If you're going to hand brush, do it carefully so that the wet paint doesn't creep under the frisket.

Paul Boyer

Paint mixing agitator. Mixing paint doesn't have to be the wrist ache it usually is. By adding several BBs to a bottle or tin, you won't have to shake it as long.

William Hogan

Masking small areas. Working on the Tamiya 1/350 scale U. S. S. *New Jersey*, I came up with a method to mask around the tiny rectangular areas on the decks. Rather than precisely measure and cut each piece of tape, I place a large piece of masking tape on a sheet of glass and randomly cut small rectangular pieces with a straightedge and knife. Then I select a piece the approximate size needed and stick it in place. Another overlapping piece can cover any remaining unmasked area.

To mask round items such as vents, I use various sizes of brass tubing as templates to cut the tape. Plastic circle templates won't do because they are easily damaged by the blade.

Alan Ernat

Color finder. If you keep your paint in a drawer and are tired of picking up every bottle to find the one you are looking for, here's an answer. Write each color's name and number on ³/₄" round stick-on labels and put one on top of each bottle cap.

Paul Frederick

Paint organizer. Have trouble finding a particular color of paint? Get organized with this inexpensive divider tray. Just use an empty kit box (use bottom inside top for strength), cut up cardboard for dividers, and arrange the paints by country, brand, or color. The flexible cardboard dividers can bend around different sized bottles.

H. Scott Edwards

Paint overspray. To remove overspray or masking leaks on clear canopies, rub on waterless hand cleaner with a cotton swab or other soft applicator. Be sure to use a nonabrasive cleaner. The plastic will be buffed to a high gloss after rinsing under water.

Nicholas R. Salerno

Paint mixer. A battery-powered cocktail mixer makes an excellent paint stirrer. Cut the blades off the shaft, drill a hole in the shaft, and use epoxy to attach a wire. Bend the end of the wire in a triangle small enough to enter the bottle of paint.

Bob Lamble

Soft figures. Painting soft-plastic figures can be frustrating because the paint does not adhere to a shiny surface. Coat the figures with super glue, which provides a flat surface that paint will stay on.

Michael Brignola

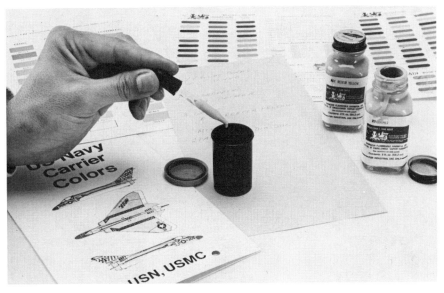

Mixing paint. I use 35 mm film canisters for mixing my paint. I measure with an eyedropper and record the amounts of paint and thinner used — if I find that a certain combination is too thick or too thin, I refer to my notes to avoid repeating the mistake.

I also record amounts of each color used when I mix paint to come up with a color not commercially available. For example, I may use ten eyedroppers of Floquil primer and add five drops of reefer yellow to come up with light gull gray. If it's too yellow I'll add two more eyedroppers of primer. If you're mixing a new color, always use the same brands of paint for compatibility and consistent results.

After getting the color I want, I thin two parts paint to one part thinner — this is just a starting point; different paints will need different ratios, so experiment to find what is best. Then I transfer the paint into the airbrush paint cup or bottle. I rarely keep leftover thinned paint; returning it to a paint bottle sometimes contaminates the remaining paint and accelerates its tendency to separate and dry. If I haven't made enough paint, I just refer to my notes and whip up a new batch.

Paul Boyer

Wheel holder. I make my own wheel holders by unfolding a paper clip. Wrap masking tape around the end of the wire to create a tight fit with large wheels — the wheel should fit snugly and not spin. The holders allow you to paint both sides of the wheel and hold them as they dry.

Justin Krauss

No-scratch scraper. Oops! You're painting the canopy frames on a model airplane and the brush just slipped onto the glass area. Don't panic. Whittle the end of a piece of sprue to a chisel point. After the paint is dry, carefully push the excess paint toward the framing. Since the sprue is no harder than the canopy, you can scrape off the paint without marring the clear plastic.

William R. Downing Jr.

Painting canopies. I paint canopy framing by hand with a fine brush. I find it easier to see the framing of the clear parts if I paint against a contrasting background — I paint a light-colored frame against a dark background and vice versa. To avoid distortion, tape or tack light or dark paper inside the canopy.

Will Reynolds

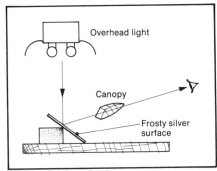

Painting canopies II. The sketch shows my method for illuminating clear canopies to make them easier to paint. I use a frosty silver surface, found on some greeting cards and TV dinner trays. The light from above reflects off the silver surface, sharply defining the canopy framing lines.

Ed Kolbush

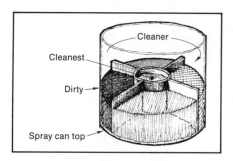

Spray can tops. Many spray paint can caps have reinforcing braces that divide them into four or more compartments. I pour paint thinner into each section and clean my brushes by removing most of the paint in the first bath and moving on to the next. The last bath is almost unpolluted. As I go full circle in the cap, the brush becomes progressively cleaner.

Kurt Sladek

Spray can tops II. I place the top of a spray can upside down on my workbench and use it to hold bottles of paint. The inner circle of plastic is just the right size for Testor, Pactra, Polly S, and other 1/2- or 5/8-ounce bottles.

James Bryan

Canopy mask. I use a combination of graphic tape and liquid masking agent to mask canopies. I apply the tape along the edges of clear areas to provide a sharp edge to the painted frame. The remaining clear areas are covered with liquid mask, such as Microscale's Micro-Mask. After it has dried, attach the canopy to the model and paint it. Use sharp tweezers to remove the tape and mask. Graphic tape comes in widths down to 1/64" that can follow most curved canopy frame lines. [See *Sources*, page 48.]

Louis J. Rucci

Bendable handles. Paintbrush handles can be removed and replaced with thick solder or other soft, bendable wire. The new handle can be crimped on or attached with super glue or epoxy. This bendable handle allows touch-up or weathering in tight areas.

Mark Savage

Acrylic cleanup. Use Windex glass cleaner for acrylic-paint cleanup — including your airbrush.

Craig Pierce

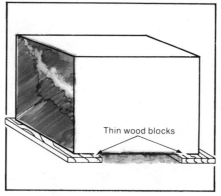

Dust free. To keep dust off a freshly painted model, I put a box over it. Plastic or metal is better than cardboard because dust gets trapped in the flaps of cardboard boxes. I prop the ends of the box up on thin pieces of wood to provide ventilation.

John Downey

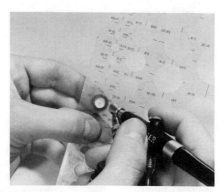

Circle template mask. An artist's circle template can be used as an instant mask when painting wheels and tires. The template has many sizes of openings that will fit just about any wheel. First paint the tire. After it has dried, mask the tire by holding the wheel firmly against the template and apply the wheel color.

Clean the tool after each use — most templates are not affected by lacquer thinner. Always paint on the shiny side for easier cleanup.

Paul Boyer

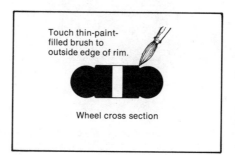

Painting wheels. Tires on wheels that have a raised rim edge are easy to paint using a fine-tip brush filled with thin dark gray flat enamel. Just touch the brush to the outside edge of the rim. The rest of the tire is easy to paint.

John Voelker

Mixing bowl. Don't throw out those plastic containers of soft margarine — they're ideal for mixing water-base paints. Place the paint container on the raised center portion of the tub and add enough water to form a shallow moat around it. This way, both paint and thinner are out of the way of your project.

John Staehle

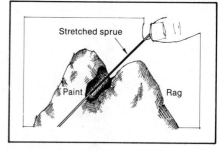

Painting stretched sprue. Here's a way to paint stretched sprue and wire before putting it on a model. Place a few drops of paint on an old rag and pull the sprue through the paint, just like wiping an automobile dipstick.

Paul Frederick

Painting tiny parts. Wrap a piece of masking tape a couple of times around the end of a round toothpick, then reverse it and wrap it back on itself a few more turns, sticky side out. I like to leave a little overhang on the end so the tape can be bent or flattened to provide a larger sticky surface. Now you can stick tiny parts to your little handle for easy painting. When you're done, stick the sharp end of the toothpick into a block of plastic foam or blob of modeling clay and let the part dry. To hold propellers and other parts that have shafts, wrap the shaft to the end of the toothpick.

Will Reynolds

Thinner saver. Drop copper (not steel wool) scrub pads into the bottom of a jar. Punch a hole in the lid, just large enough for the tip of your airbrush, then put the lid on the jar. After using the airbrush, fill the reservoir with thinner and spray through the hole in the lid. The scrub pads trap particles of paint, and the thinner trickles to the bottom of the jar, where it can be poured off and used again. Stick to one brand of thinner: Incompatible types will turn gummy.

David Blocker

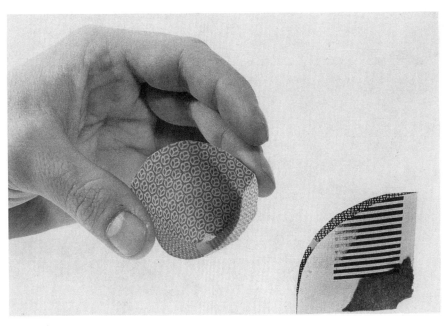

Disposable funnel. If you need to transfer paint from one container to another, or if you just need to strain the paint, you can cut a small funnel out of an envelope. Cut the envelope about 2″ from the corner and then cut off the tip. When you squeeze the edges, the corner opens up into a cone. For a filter, use white glue to attach a piece of nylon stocking material over the opening.

Ed Kolbush

Elmer's mask. I use Elmer's Craft Bond I as a liquid canopy mask. Simply brush it on straight from the container. There may be small spots where the glue won't stick due to dirt or oil. Don't worry; just wait for the first coat to dry, then apply a second coat. After painting, simply peel off the glue.

Chuck Hammerick

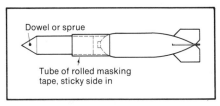

Dowel or sprue

Tube of rolled masking tape, sticky side in

Masking bomb tips. Here's an easy way to mask small compound curves such as bombs, rockets, or fuel tanks. Paint the nose color first, then make a tube of masking tape, rolled to the proper diameter with the sticky side in. The tube should be rolled in two or three layers for rigidity. Make sure the end of the tube is cut cleanly, then press it gently in place. Push the dowel into a block of plastic foam or hold it in a spring-type clothespin while painting the rest of the part.

John G. Voelker

Paint and mount figures. Carefully drill a hole in the figure's foot and glue a styrene rod or stretched sprue inside (larger figures may require a metal rod). Trimmed to a convenient length, the rod can then be held in a vise or clamp while painting the figure. This also facilitates mounting the figure on a base; drill a hole for the rod, then glue the figure in place.

Michael Chevalier

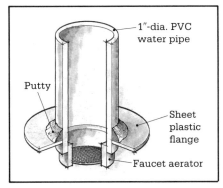

1″-dia. PVC water pipe

Putty

Sheet plastic flange

Faucet aerator

Paint strainer. I had some surplus 1″ PVC pipe — from one of my wife's "honey-do" jobs — and a leftover faucet aerator. The aerator fits snugly inside the PVC pipe, but I sealed mine with putty. I place this on top of my Badger paint bottles and it strains the paint as I pour.

Wayne A. Denny

Paint cleanup. Get more paint on your hands than your model? I keep a container of "Wet Ones" moist towelettes on my workbench. A light wipe takes paint right off, and the towelettes smell better than thinner. They also remove small painting mistakes from your model.

Bob Rush

Removable tape. I use Scotch Magic Plus removable transparent tape to mask my models. Its low-tack adhesive won't pull up fragile finishes like Metalizer and Liqu-a-plate. It's not the best on compound curves and heavy surface detail but it's excellent on straight lines. Look for it in office and art-supply stores.

D. H. Minton

Tinting glass. I found an easy way to tint cockpit glass on my model airplanes. I thin Polly S Gloss (PF70) with rubbing alcohol and add a drop of food coloring. This mixture airbrushes well. Sometimes more than one coat is necessary to achieve the proper tint. Always be sure to let the tint dry between coats. You can wash off mistakes with water.

Bob Ferreira

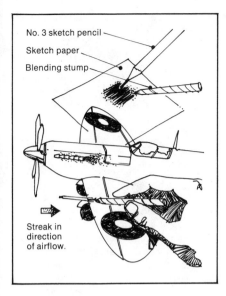

No. 3 sketch pencil
Sketch paper
Blending stump

Streak in direction of airflow.

Pencil smoke stains. I have trouble applying exhaust and gun smoke stains with an airbrush, so I use this method: Rub the side of a No. 3 sketch pencil lead on a piece of paper until you have a pile of black powder. Rub the tip of a paper artist's blending stump into the powder and gradually build up the smoke stains on the model, streaked in line with the airstream over the wings and fuselage. A little color goes a long way, so work slowly. Mistakes can be removed with soap and warm water or a vinyl eraser. These items can be found at art-supply stores.

Michael Kane

Not-so-heavy weather. Paint on real armored vehicles is hardly indestructible, but this weathering effect is often overdone on armor models. The paint rarely chips off in flakes (as is sometimes the case with aircraft); the actual appearance is more of a scuffing, and occurs in those areas where crew traffic is heaviest — around hatches and fueling points. In most cases the effect is so subtle that it would be barely visible in 1/35 scale. While you don't want to ignore it, don't overdo it either.

Using a mixture of silver and black, dry the brush almost completely by wiping most of the paint off on a piece of paper, then scrub the area with the dry brush. The remaining nearly dry pigment will produce a realistic worn area.

Shep Paine

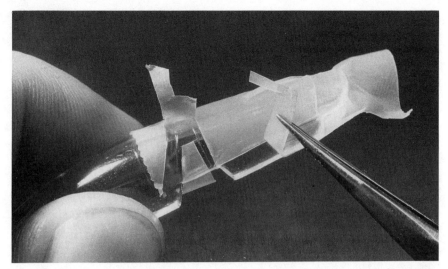

Masking. I use Scotch Magic Mending tape, the frosty tape in the green plaid dispenser. It's thin and sticks tight to plastic. Apply pieces of tape to cover the canopy glass and framing. Use a fresh hobby knife and carefully cut along the frame lines, making sure the blade cuts through the tape (you won't have to press hard). Peel the tape from the framing by lifting the ends with the knife and grabbing them with tweezers. When you're finished, the canopy should look clear on all the frames and frosty on all the glass areas.

You're not quite through — cover the *inside* of the canopy with tape. Just before you spray, burnish the edges of the tape so the paint won't creep under it. Peel off the masking an hour after painting — any longer and you run the risk of the paint becoming brittle and chipping on the frame edges.

Paul Boyer

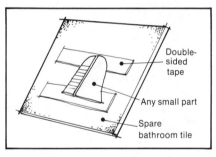

Double-sided tape

Any small part

Spare bathroom tile

Painting small parts. When I have small parts to paint, I attach them with double-sided tape to a spare ceramic bathroom wall tile. The tile is impervious to paint, heavy enough so it won't blow away, and small enough to move into a spray booth and set aside. Best of all, it keeps fingers off the freshly painted parts. Use lacquer thinner for cleanup.

Steve Willocks

Coloring water-base paints. Do you have a water-base color that isn't quite the shade you want? Try adding a little food coloring. It makes light colors darker without making them look dirty, as black paint sometimes does.

Eric Wagner

Fine paint applicator. Applying tiny amounts of paint is difficult even with the finest brushes, so try a sharp hobby-knife blade instead. Pick up a bit of paint on the tip of the blade and transfer it to the model.

Art Baba

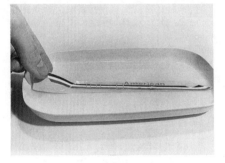

Frozen dinner tray. Armour's Dinner Classics come in a heat-resistant plastic tray that I use to hold water when decaling. It is long enough for most decals and shallow enough so that I don't have to roll up my sleeves to get that tiny stencil from the bottom.

Paul Boyer

Neat lines. To get sharper trim lines, spray a light coat of clear on the model after the major color and trim masking have been applied. Then apply the trim color. The clear coat keeps the trim color from seeping under the mask by sealing the tape line.

Tim Cislo

Brush cleaner. Don't throw away small paintbrushes clogged with dried enamel paint. Just dip them in IPS Weld-On #3 plastic cement and wipe them on a cloth. After repeating the process a few times, the paint should peel off completely without damaging the bristles.

David Krakow

Cast-metal texture. Many tank parts, such as the gun mantlet on a T-34 and the turret on an M48, are made of cast metal, which has a rough finish. However, most kit parts have a smooth finish. Here's one way to achieve a cast-metal look on styrene parts: Gently brush tiny quantities of model airplane dope such as Pactra Aerogloss onto the plastic, let the dope soften the plastic for a few minutes, then stipple the plastic with a stiff-bristled disposable brush, imparting a rough, textured effect.

Obviously, the more dope you use and the longer you let it work, the heavier the effect will be. If you overdo it, sand down the surface slightly. It's best to go slowly and learn through practice when to stop.

Warning — dope contains powerful solvents that eat styrene. It is easy to ruin an expensive kit, so practice this technique on scrap plastic or an old model before tackling your latest project. Keep in mind, too, that as with most modeling techniques, it's better to be too subtle than to go too far and end up with a curdled mess.

Dave Musikoff

Drawing pencils. The next time you are in an art-supply store, check out their stock of colored drawing pencils. These look just like regular lead pencils, but the fillers come in every shade imaginable.

The most useful color I've found is silver. Sharpened like a regular pencil, the silver pencil can be used to give realistic highlights to any object that's supposed to be metal.

Try painting a machine gun a dark shade of gunmetal, let it dry, and then carefully touch the raised details, the corners, and other areas with the pencil. With a little practice, you can simulate wear and tear effectively; one advantage of the pencil over trying the same thing with paint is that if you mess up or overdo the effect, you can simply wet the area with water and rub away mistakes.

Military vehicle modelers may want to buy a white pencil and try their hands at simulating chalked-on slogans, and other markings often seen on such vehicles.

Dave Musikoff

Plastic wrap and bag mask. Plastic food wrap and food storage bags make ideal masking agents. Simply wrap the plastic around the areas you want to protect. Use masking tape or frisket film for the actual color demarcation line. The plastic wrap clings by static electricity, and the plastic bag can be sealed with tape, rubber bands, or pipe cleaners.

Burr Angle and Paul Boyer

Don't throw it away! As expensive as good-quality paintbrushes are, they still must be replaced when they become frayed and worn. Rather than throwing them away, keep them for those unusual jobs, like rough groundwork or, with a little trimming with a hobby knife, for applying dapple camouflage schemes.

Jack Clark

No tinted lenses here. Most modelers know it's best to wear a filter mask or respirator when spray painting. It's also a good idea for those who wear soft contact lenses to wear inexpensive plastic safety goggles to protect the lenses from contamination.

Michael Denney

Removing chrome. Ferric chloride (also known as etchant) removes chrome plating without damaging plastic. You can buy it at Radio Shack (part No. 276-1935). Soak the parts in a full-strength solution, wait (anywhere from 5 minutes to ½ hour), rinse them in *cold* water, and scrub them with an old toothbrush. *Caution!* Ferric chloride is both corrosive and poisonous; use rubber gloves, goggles, and a disposable container.

Graeme McEachren

Nail polish remover. I clean my paintbrushes with nail polish remover. It cleans the brushes well, plus it leaves a conditioning residue on the brush hair.

Chris Morris

Airbrush trick. Before using your double-action airbrush, remove the needle and rub it on your forehead. Skin oil keeps paint from sticking to the needle. This may sound like voodoo, but it really works! *Mw. Mac Kay*

Soda straw. Acrylic paint will last longer if you blow into the paint with a soda straw before closing the bottle. It sounds strange, but there is a scientific basis: Bubbling breath through the paint displaces oxygen with carbon dioxide from your lungs. Oxygen causes paint to oxidize, skin over, and solidify.
M. Mac Kay

Tinted windows. Almost any flat or slightly curved canopy can be tinted with commercial artist's color films. These are gummed-back, transparent acetate sheets that come in many colors, available at art- or drafting-supply stores. Brands to look for are Chartpak or Zip-a-Tone; be sure to get the glossy surface. Cut a piece slightly larger than needed, peel off the plastic backing, and burnish the tint onto the inside of the canopy with your finger. If it doesn't work the first time, peel it off and try again. [See *Sources*, page 48.]
Pete Harlem

Airbrush cleaner. I clean small parts in my airbrush with a Butler dental brush called "Proxabrush." It comes in three sizes, and it's available at most drugstores for about $2. First, I disassemble the airbrush and soak it in lacquer thinner for a few hours. Don't soak any rubber washers or plastic parts as the lacquer thinner will dissolve them.

Fred Amos

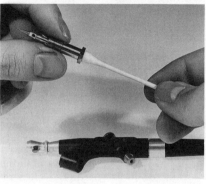

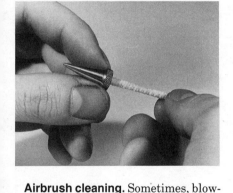

Airbrush cleaning. Sometimes, blowing thinner through an airbrush isn't enough to thoroughly clean it. If I'm spraying one color after another in one sitting, I'll take the airbrush apart and clean it after every three colors. Take the needle housing (the tip) apart and inspect the inside. If there is hard, crusty buildup, soak the parts (tip up) in a small jar of lacquer thinner for an hour. Clean the rear portion of the tip with a cotton swab and pipe cleaner soaked in lacquer thinner. The front portion should be cleaned carefully with a thin pipe cleaner. Don't jam it into the tip; the metal at the tip is thin and easily damaged by the wire in the pipe cleaner. Also, clean out the siphon in the paint jar or cup. Now you're ready to move on to the next color.

Paul Boyer

Touch-up paints. Check hardware stores and auto, truck, and farm machinery equipment dealers' parts departments for authentic, factory touch-up paints. The colors can be used from the spray can or can be sprayed into a bottle for use in an airbrush.

Mark Savage

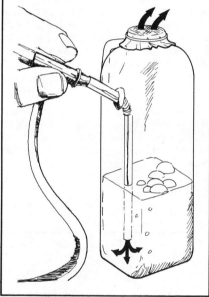

Indoor airbrushing. Unless you have a spray booth, spraying thinner through your airbrush will fill a room with noxious fumes. All you need to solve this problem is a gallon milk jug and plastic tubing. Poke a hole in the jug near the bottom of the handle and insert the tubing (a flexible drinking straw is ideal) so the end of the tubing is at the bottom of the jug. Affix the tubing with epoxy and fill one-third of the jug with water and liquid detergent (a 50-50 mix). After airbrushing, spray excess paint and thinner through the tubing; the paint and thinner will emerge from the submerged end of the tube, creating a foam that prevents most of the fumes from escaping. Additionally, you can put a filter (a nylon sock or paper towel) over the mouth of the jug, trapping more harmful particulates. Cap the container when you're through, take it outside, then uncap it and let the fumes go out there. Change the detergent solution regularly.

Lee Coll

Paint stripper. I found a safe and effective way to remove flat paint from plastic models. I mix two to three cups of trisodium phosphate (TSP) to a gallon of hot tap water and add one cup of bleach and a small bottle of household cleaner (such as 409 or Fantastik). I soak the parts overnight, then make a paste of TSP and hot water and scrub it onto the plastic with an old toothbrush. Although this is easier on skin than oven cleaners, I still recommend rubber gloves and eye protection.

Fred Meccia

Cheaper paint. Tired of buying modeling paints at high prices? The next time you're at an arts and crafts store, look at the paints for ceramics. Read the labels closely and you'll find that some are acrylic paints. The colors may read "apple green" or "eggshell blue," but you may end up paying only 99 cents for two ounces — and I'll bet your airbrush won't know the difference.

John Staehle

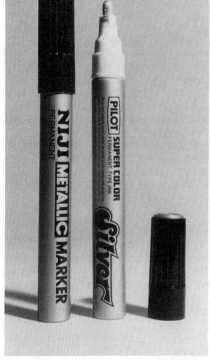

Metallic markers. I have found something in my local art store that has turned out to be quite a help in finishing my model cars. It's called a metallic marker. The markers are made by Niji and Pilot, come in silver, gold, and copper, and broad or fine points. The ink is permanent.

I use the markers to highlight small chrome areas on my cars and trucks; they're much neater than brushes.

The metallic quality of the ink falls somewhere between the silver paints I use and Bare-Metal Foil.

Brian O'Leary

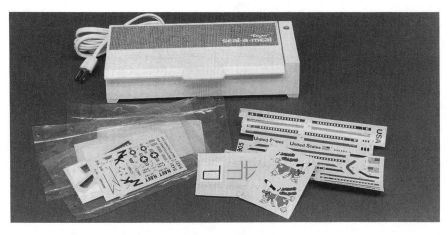

Saving decals. Changes in temperature and humidity are the great enemies of decals. Often the decals in a kit that is only two or three years old will be brittle and impossible to apply.

To protect decals that don't come sealed in their own plastic bags, and to save leftover decals for use years from now, I seal the sheets in the same plastic pouches that we use in the kitchen for freezing homegrown vegetables.

I use the Dazey "Seal-a-Meal" brand of bags and heat-seal machine; similar devices are available from 3M and other firms.

Sealing the decals in the pouches, make sure that you include a list of the contents, or that you can readily see just what decals are in which bag. Incidentally, while the pouches will maintain steady humidity, temperature is another story. I keep the sealed pouches in a box in my basement, where the temperature stays within ten degrees of 65 degrees Fahrenheit year-round.

Bob Hayden

Cheap air. A cheap source of compressed air for your airbrush is available right under your feet! For around $7 you can purchase a foot-powered pump used to inflate tires or air mattresses. Along with a 160 psi tank (which doesn't take up much room), your air supply is unlimited. It's good exercise, too.

I pump mine up to about 40 psi, enough to spray one color on an average-size model. Standard brass fittings will work on the tank to connect the hose and serve as reducers.

John Staehle

Paint planning. Kit instructions usually include line drawings of the model. Make copies of the drawings, then experiment with the camouflage or paint scheme. Visualizing the result of your color scheme can save paint and help you avoid regrets.

Randall J. Guenin

Decal blotter. A sponge-tip makeup applicator from the cosmetic counter of a department store is perfect for blotting water and setting solution from decals. It has a short plastic handle with a round, fine-textured sponge on the end. The makeup sponge will soak up many times its weight just by pressing straight down on the decal. Decals won't stick to the sponge, and by pressing vertically, distortion and cracking are avoided. They are especially helpful when decaling corrugated or concave surfaces.

T. E. Bell

Paint hulk. Instead of test spraying on a rag or cardboard, I use an old model to get the right paint consistency and spray pattern. Using my old "paint hulk" helps me avoid disasters and gives me a better idea of what the paint will look like before I apply it to my latest creation. It's also handy for determining whether various types of paint are compatible or whether a gloss or matte overcoat will change the colors.

Dave Musikoff

Polishing cloth. Shoe-buffing cloths often found in hotel rooms are useful. They're good for buffing metal finishes, polishing canopies, and are relatively lint free. Mitt-shaped ones can be used as gloves to prevent fingerprints.

T. E. Bell

Airbrush leaks. Leaks in your airbrush from worn or stripped threads? Seal them with beeswax.

D. L. Mulligan

Metal eye shadow. To achieve a realistic worn-metal surface on painted areas, I rub on different shades of silver eye shadow. The package my wife bought five years ago has enough left in it today for hundreds of models. Many brands come with a sponge applicator that conforms to irregular surfaces. The oily texture of these products ensures they will adhere to painted parts. *George Kendall II*

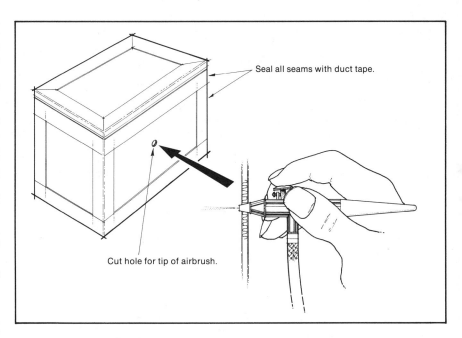

Seal all seams with duct tape.

Cut hole for tip of airbrush.

Antipollution device. Here's an inexpensive and effective way to cut down on workshop air pollution. Select a medium-size box, preferably with a separate lid rather than flaps, and seal the top and all seams with duct tape. Cut a small hole just large enough to accept the nozzle of your airbrush.

When you blow thinner through your airbrush to clean it, blow it into the box, then tape over the hole. After the painting session, take the box outdoors, uncover the hole, and let the fumes out. Keep flames and smoking materials away from the box.

David Hamilton

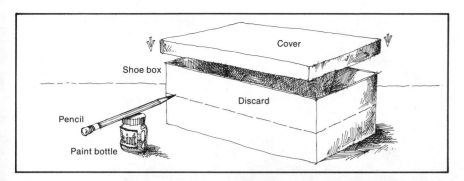

Cover
Shoe box
Discard
Pencil
Paint bottle

Paint storage. I take an ordinary shoe box and, using a paint bottle as a guide, draw a line around the bottom with a pencil. I cut off the upper part and place my paints inside the box and use the original cover. I can stack nearly twice as many of these shortened boxes in the same space as standard boxes. *Dick Sirola*

The holed decal. Keep decals from silvering: Use a pin to poke holes in the decal before applying it. This allows setting solution or solvent to get under the decal. *Gary Goldblatt*

Pastel applicator. I cut a round, stiff-bristled brush to use as a pastel applicator. The short, rounded profile allows me to stipple the pastel chalk dust onto the model with pleasing results. I cut down Nos. 0, 1, and 2 size brushes for my 1/72 scale models. *Will Reynolds*

Pastels. When weathering with pastel chalks, apply them as usual, then streak them with a damp brush. This gives the subject an excellent weathered look and helps the fine powder adhere to the model. *Bill Wells*

Realistic rust. Spray the object that you want to paint with red lead primer (for example, rust inhibitor), then a light coat of flat black. Applying the black coat while the base coat is still wet produces an interesting effect. Try varying the distance from which you spray, too. *Christopher Breeze*

Detail cosmetician. I've tried just about everything for fine paint detailing on ships, planes, armor, and figures, and with the help of my three teenage daughters, I've found something that works for me — makeup! It's inexpensive and available at any cosmetic counter. Eye shadow and face makeup come in many shades that work well as brushed-on highlights. I seal them with a spray of clear flat. You might want to get your own supply — borrowing your wife's or daughter's may get you in hot water! *Larry Dever*

Blending stumps. When weathering, Rub 'n Buff or pastels are easier to apply if you use an artist's blending stump. They're available at art-supply stores. *Dick Hirdes*

Decal storage. Office supply stores carry clear vinyl sheet protectors that are ideal for storing decals and their instruction sheets. The vinyl protectors are sealed on three sides, keep out excess humidity, and keep the decals flat. *Mark Elder*

Water trap and air filter. Many auto part stores carry the CR brand "Pro-Fuel" fuel filters. Get one that will fit a 1/4″ fuel line, cut your airbrush hose apart, and force the hose ends onto the filter fittings. It'll be a tight squeeze, but don't use any lubricant — it could end up in your paint job. Put a few drops of super glue on the hose braid to keep it from unraveling, and put a small fuel line hose clamp over the hose at the fittings. *Jim Ireland*

Paint siphon. If your airbrush paint siphon tube is hopelessly cracked or clogged, replace it with an empty ink tube found in inexpensive ball point pens like Bic. The plastic ink tube can be cut to the right size for your paint bottle. *Nubbin Galendez*

Fuel stains. After weathering my armor models, I use a toothpick to apply a small drop of the reddish clear liquid from the top of an unstirred bottle of Pactra Hull Red (IN61) to the fuel filler ports. It looks like a stain from spilled fuel — shiny and slightly red. *Joe Hively*

Painting warm-up. Before painting a figure, go to your leftovers and pick out the worst figure you can find. Begin by painting that figure. You'll be surprised what a little warm-up can do for you! *Jack Clark*

Decals and bacon. I keep my decals in a Tupperware Bacon Keeper. It's big enough to hold dozens of the largest aftermarket decals. The nearly airtight seal keeps out harmful humidity. *Brian Slipper*

Decal preserver. To keep decals from chipping and cracking, apply a light coat of clear (either gloss or flat) over the entire decal sheet. Remember, this means that you have to cut out each decal to apply it. *Jay Zvolanek*

More metal. Here is a way to make realistic gunmetal on weapons and other items. First paint the part with Pactra scale black or Floquil gunmetal. Then apply powdered graphite; it comes in a two-ounce tube and can be found at hardware stores. I dispense the graphite powder on paper, rub my thumb and forefinger in it, then rub the graphite onto the areas I want highlighted, such as barrels and hardware. Wipe away excess graphite with a rag, or touch up with paint.

If you don't want to get your fingers in the graphite you can use a cotton swab. For 54 mm figures and 1/35 scale tanks, wrap cotton around a wood cocktail stick to make a small applicator. Overspray with a flat finish, and the graphite takes on a scale metal color. *Joe Hively*

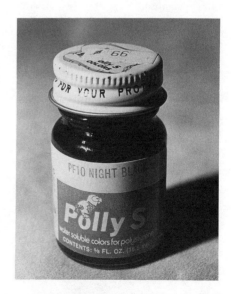

Black wash. A thin black wash represents stains on your weathered models. Unfortunately, most black inks take on a reddish or bluish hue when water is added. However, Polly S Night Black (PF10) stays black even when diluted. *Burr Angle*

4. Detailing

Vinyl roofs. To make textured vinyl roofs for model cars, apply a coat of model airplane dope to the plastic. Dope softens the plastic and allows you to stipple the texture with a stiff brush. Be careful to keep the dope off areas you don't want to texture. Most vinyl roofs have seams where the sections of material overlap. These can be simulated with thin strips of paper attached with super glue. After the dope dries, you can paint the roof.

Keith L. Pieper

Model car seat belts. I cut bookbinding repair tape into strips for seat belts in my 1/25 scale cars. It's textured, it comes in many colors, and with wire or photoetched buckles it looks realistic.

Bill Gebhard

Brighter foil. Bare-Metal Foil, a thin, adhesive-backed metal foil, is an excellent chrome replacement. Polishing with tissue paper gives it an even brighter sheen, and the extra rubbing makes the foil adhere better. [See *Sources*, page 48.]

Chuck Dela Rosa

Scale mohair. Plain paper towel replicates mohair for the interior of old-style cars like my Ertl/AMT '40 Ford. To imitate headlining, pad it with quilted cotton. Cut the paper into strips for a segmented look.

Stephen Lipken

Car carpet. If you like to detail model cars, check your local hardware store or home improvement center for velour contact. Its adhesive backing makes this "carpet" easy to install

Brett Mills

Close, but . . . Scale wood can be obtained from a tobacco store: The thin wood liners of a cigar box make excellent veneer for station wagons, interiors, etc. Finish with a clear gloss, or stain to the desired color.

Stephen Lipken

Car seats. Here's how to get realistic vinyl car seats. Upholster the plastic seats with regular masking tape, being careful to correctly align the grain. Add piping made from wire glued on with super glue. Paint the seats with gloss enamel. Just before the paint loses its tackiness, touch the raised areas with your finger. This dulls the sheen and gives it a worn look.

Edward Zarate

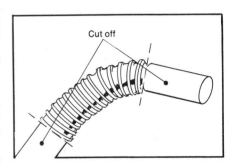

Engine hoses. Ribbed elbows on bendable plastic straws make good hoses for engine detailing. Add the ribbed section to your engine, paint it along with the engine, give it a dirty wash and some dry-brushing, and you'll have a realistic hose.

Alvin E. Hubert

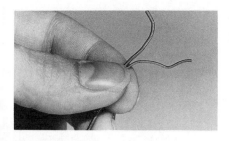

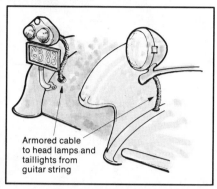

Armored cable to head lamps and taillights from guitar string

Guitar strings. "Round wound" guitar strings are wire wrapped around wire. These strings make terrific-looking oxygen hoses for aircraft cockpits, or armored electrical cable for large scale autos. It's easier to bend the string if the center wire is removed.

Giuseppe Bertocchi

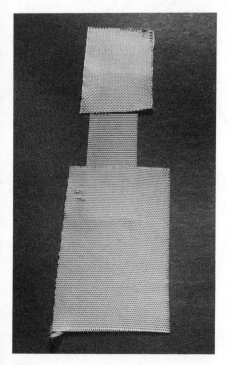

Tape for seat belts. Scotch Glass Cloth Electrical Tape, available from electrician's supply stores, is ideal for making seat belts. The tape comes in three thread patterns (top to bottom): No. 27, good for large scales, No. 69 for medium scales, and No. 13 for small scales. Different widths are available. The tape doesn't fray if it's cut clean, and it's sticky enough to hold itself to seats.

Jim Steel

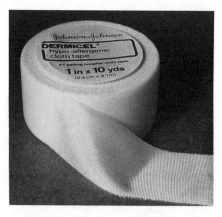

Realistic fabric. Johnson and Johnson makes a hypoallergenic cloth tape called Dermicel, a tightly woven fabric with an adhesive backing. It's easy to cut and paint, and it makes good-looking fabric for seat belts and shoulder harnesses.

Mark Lewis

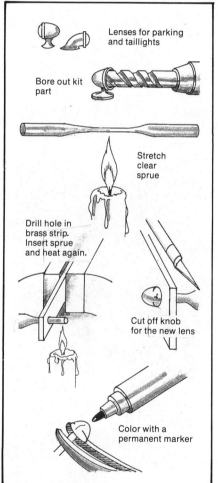

Lenses for parking and taillights

Bore out kit part

Stretch clear sprue

Drill hole in brass strip. Insert sprue and heat again.

Cut off knob for the new lens

Color with a permanent marker

Car lenses. Here's a tip that adds colored lenses to auto lights. Bore or drill out the molded-in lens area. Heat and stretch clear sprue to a size smaller than you need, insert the sprue through a hole drilled in a piece of brass, and heat it again until a knob is formed. Cut off the knob and color it with a permanent marker. Fit the new lens into the bored-out kit part.

Giuseppe Bertocchi

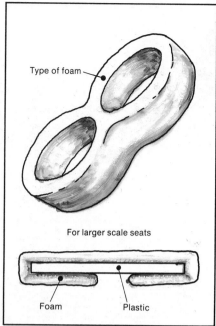

Type of foam

For larger scale seats

Foam   Plastic

Leather seat cushions. A good material for making leather seat cushions is plastic foam packing material. Cut a piece of the foam, flatten it with your fingers, cut it to size, and attach it with white glue. Paint the cushion a leather color, then dry-brush with a lighter color; this highlights the cracks and creases and gives it a worn-leather look.

For larger scales, first cut a piece of scrap plastic slightly smaller than the cushion. Wrap a piece of the flattened foam around the plastic as if you were upholstering a chair seat, and fasten it from underneath.

Kevin Hensel

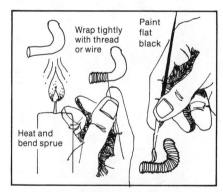

Wrap tightly with thread or wire

Paint flat black

Heat and bend sprue

Realistic radiator hoses. To make realistic radiator hoses, bend plastic sprue over a candle to the shape you need. Next, wrap the sprue with heavy thread or thin-gauge wire, then paint the hose flat black and cut it to fit your model.

Clark Allen

Twist ties. The wire in bread-bag twist ties is perfect for radio wires, barbed wire, fuel lines, and so forth. Simply strip the paper or plastic coating away.

T. Short

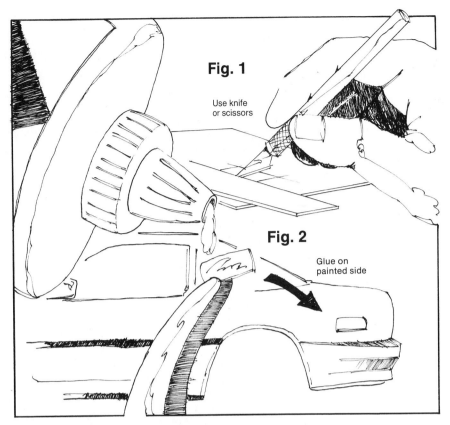

Fig. 1

Use knife or scissors

Fig. 2

Glue on painted side

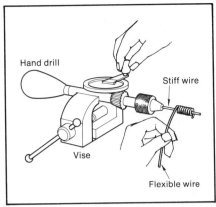

Hand drill

Stiff wire

Vise

Flexible wire

Coiled wire. Here's another way to make realistic oxygen hoses and other coiled hoses for models. Place a hand drill in a vise and mount a stiff wire in the chuck. Wrap flexible wire around the stiff wire as you turn the drill's wheel. Slide the coil off the wire and paint it.

Giuseppe Bertocchi

Lights fantastic. Here's a neat idea for simulating running lights or CRT screens. Using a *translucent* color, paint a thin piece of clear plastic (.01″ thickness works well). Apply a coat of chrome or silver over the base coat. Cut the painted plastic to shape, Fig. 1, and apply white glue to the silver-painted side, Fig. 2. Put in place and admire!

Brian Sturton

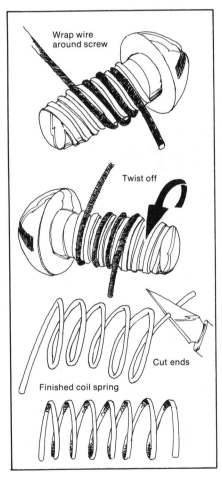

Wrap wire around screw

Twist off

Cut ends

Finished coil spring

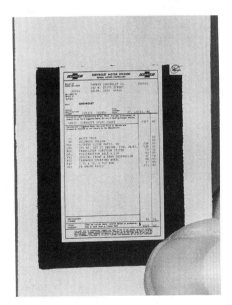

Sticker shrink. Auto swap meets are great places to buy auto accessories you can use for model cars. In addition to brochures, look for blank window price stickers. You can find books that list the code numbers and prices of all the options available on a certain car. Type in the options you installed in your model car, then reduce it on a copier to the scale of your model. This example is 1/8 scale — smaller copies are almost unreadable, but still look great!

Daryl Fink

1/12 scale racing helmet. Tamiya's 1/12 scale Ferrari 312B kit contains a driver figure with a nice helmet. If you don't like to have figures in your cars, but do like the helmet, cut off the figure's head (it's painless!), grind out the neck, and paint the back of the visor black to simulate tinting. Paint the outside of the helmet any color you choose.

J. Robert Young

Scale maps. Add realism to figures in dioramas by providing them with scale maps. Get part of a real road map and reduce it to scale on a photocopy machine. For a finishing touch, draw color on the scale map.

Bill Wells

Coiled spring. Wrap fine wire around a screw, following the threads. Twist the wire off the screw, trim the ends of the wire, and you have a small-scale coiled spring. *Eric Peterson*

Leather detail. Use gloss writing paper for webbing, straps, and rifle slings; it's cheap, and it's easy to cut and bend.

Paul Adams

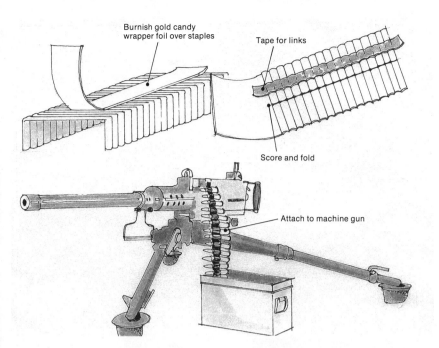

Burnish gold candy wrapper foil over staples

Tape for links

Score and fold

Attach to machine gun

Ammo belts. Gold foil found in candy wrappers can be used to simulate machine gun ammunition belts. First, burnish the gold foil over a cartridge of staples; this produces a relief pattern similar to the shell casings. Before removing the foil from the staples, press on a thin piece of black- or silver-painted tape to simulate the links. Next, apply a thin black wash to accentuate the relief. Cut the foil to twice the width needed, lightly score down the middle, apply white glue to the back, and fold it over. The white glue fills each round, allowing the belt to be flexed without destroying detail. Hang the belt from the machine gun with a realistic sag. This technique is good for ammo belts up to 1/48 scale.

David Krakow

Shim ruler. An easy way to scribe straight lines on irregularly shaped pieces is to use thin shim brass as a sturdy but flexible ruler. I use brass shims made by K&S Engineering. [See *Sources*, page 48.]

Blair Yoshida

Textured foil. The embossed foil wrapper on Klondike ice-cream bars can be used as insulation material in spacecraft and science-fiction models.

Mark Savage

Staples. Common staples make grab handles or steps on ship, truck, armor, or industrial models. Attach them with super glue.

Mark Savage

Towing shackles. To model heavy towing shackles on AFV models, use 15-amp fuse wire and shape it to fit. It's easier to bend than plastic rod.

Paul Adams

Ribbon treads. Unhappy with kit-supplied tread for 1/72 scale tanks, I came up with my own tread material — gift-wrapping ribbon! It bonds with super glue, and when it's weathered it looks realistic.

Jay Zvolanek

Foil tread plate. The foil from Parkay Margarine has texture similar to tread plate for 1/35 scale models.

Ernesto Cabrera

Simulating helmet netting. Stretch a piece of old panty hose over a helmet. The more you stretch, the bigger the netting openings will be. Clamp the excess with self-closing tweezers, then apply liquid cement, making sure to get the edges. Trim the edges when they're dry, then paint. Dry-brushing brings out the texture.

Robert Martinez

M3 ring mounts. You can make M3 ring mounts for 1/35 and 1/32 scale truckks and armored cars with the lid from a 35 mm film canister. Using a hobby knife, cut off the outer rim of the lid. Clean up the inside of the ring with sandpaper. As a bonus, you'll find that many canisters have a rim that looks like the rollers of a gun cradle.

Robert E. Materelli Jr.

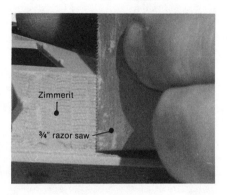

Zimmerit

3/4" razor saw

Easy Zimmerit. It's easy to model Zimmerit with epoxy putty and a 3/4" razor saw. On large sections, apply a bead of putty to one end of a panel, then drag the putty with the saw blade. On smaller sections, apply a thin coat of putty, then groove it. If the putty starts to set, soften it with liquid cement.

Glen Phillips

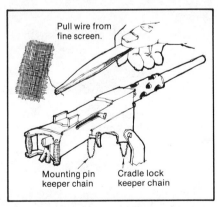

Pull wire from fine screen.

Mounting pin keeper chain

Cradle lock keeper chain

Keeper chains. To model the keeper chains retaining mounting pins of .50 caliber machine guns and the thumbscrews of jeep windshields, I pull a single strand of wire from a piece of superfine screen. Just bend the wire into a half loop and super glue it in place. Paint and dry-brush it to add the finishing touches.

Jack Clark

The ways of Zimmerit. There are several ways to simulate Zimmerit on tanks. Use a hot knife and a hobby-knife blade to melt the pattern into the plastic; practice on sheet styrene first. Use a light touch so that you don't put a hole in the plastic.

Another way is to spread filler putty on a small area and score in the pattern with a knife while the putty is still soft. Work in small areas so that the putty doesn't set up as you work. This same method can be used with spackling compound, available in hardware stores. I prefer the premixed type. Make sure the model is clean and free of grease and oil, since the compound won't stick to oily plastic.

Glenn Kreinus

Bedrolls. To make bedrolls and camouflage netting, soak paper tissue or gauze in diluted white glue and roll or fold it to shape. Let it dry completely before painting.

Justin Krauss

Florist's sandbags. Florist's clay is slightly harder than modeling clay, nonhardening, dark green — and it's cheap! For a dollar at my local nursery, I can buy enough to make 200 1/32 scale sandbags.

Use a hobby knife or old butter knife to cut the clay into strips about 2″ x 2″, then cut off and shape individual bags. Coat each bag with a mixture of white glue and fine sand to give it a rough texture. Spray on a coat of khaki paint and a brown wash. Now tie the sandbags on your tank, or stack them in your artillery emplacement.

Use the clay to make cannonballs, bricks — almost anything!

Edward John Wojcik

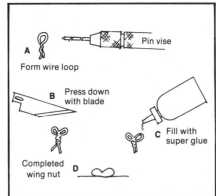

Wing nuts. To make 1/32 scale wing nuts, wrap fine wire around a drill bit to form a loop, press the center of the loop down with a knife blade until it meets the bottom of the loop, then fill the gaps with super glue. Cut the "nut" from the wire, attach it to the model, and paint it.

Barry Lank

Not white glue. Do you use white glue to build up details such as buttons or rivets? Make your job easier; use glue made for dark wood. This glue is dark brown and easier to see than white glue. Of course, you might want to use this dark glue for diorama landscaping instead.

Roy S. Goodman

Steel tow cables. Tow cables for tank models can be made easily and realistically from florist wire. Take three pieces of wire and insert one end of the bunch in a vise, the other in a hand drill. By winding wire this way you can achieve the tightness you want and the strands will be wound uniformly. Make the end loops with wire solder or anything else that works.

Walt Kupson

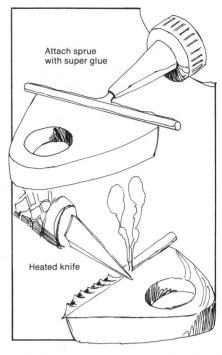

Weld seams. In large scales (1/25 and larger), use stretched sprue to make realistic weld seams. Cut sprue to the size of the seam and super glue it in place. Detail the seam with a hot knife.

Barry Lank

Color film transparencies. I can get great lenses for periscopes or range finders simply by photographing a clear, blue sky with slide film. Shooting red or amber lights gives you nice lens material, too.

Curtis Townsend

Wing walks. Cut strips of fine-grit sandpaper, paint them black, and attach them to the wings.

Bucky Bradshaw

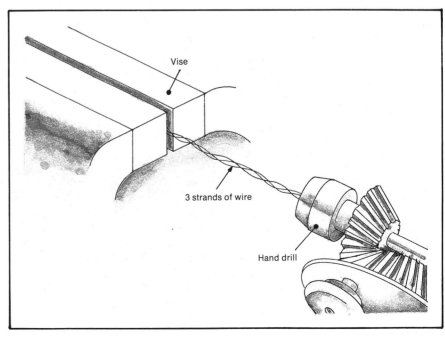

Scale towing cables. If you are looking for a simple but effective way to make authentic-looking steel towing cables for military vehicles, buy a package of model airplane control-line lead-out wire. It's distributed by the Perfect Parts Co. and by Sig Manufacturing Co. in 4' to 6' lengths and diameters of 0.021" and 0.027"; both sizes contain seven stainless steel strands. [See *Sources*, page 48.] The larger diameter is ideal for 1/35 and 1/32 scale models; the smaller looks good on models down to about 1/48 scale.

New wire is shiny and stiff, but this isn't a problem. Cut a piece the length you need (I always cut it just a bit longer to be safe), grip the wire with pliers, and heat it over a burner on your stove until the wire glows red-hot. This takes the temper out of the metal, making it soft and easily bendable — and the wire turns a realistic rusty-brown.

The next step is to drill out the cable end-connectors supplied with most armor kits and insert the wire. Secure it with a small drop of super glue. Then bend and twist the wire into position.

Dave Musikoff

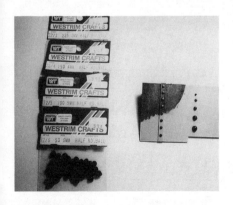

Rivets. You can buy small, plastic half-round balls at craft stores to use for rivets on large scale models: They come in 3 mm, 4 mm, 5 mm, and 6 mm sizes. Look for Westrim Crafts [see *Sources*, page 48]. Simply spear one with a sharp hobby knife, apply a little glue to the flat side, and place it on the model. A little sanding and paint will cover the mark from the knife.

Karl Machtanz

Ejection-seat handles. Small loops from used staples make good ejection-seat handles. Apply them with super glue or epoxy. *Peter Vasilion*

Sheet moss. Replicate foliage camouflage on tanks and military vehicles with florist's sheet moss, also called decorator moss. A fine-textured, dried, natural moss, it's dark brown-green, but it can be tinted any color with Rit household dye. Attach it with white glue.

Shep Paine

Chain link fence. American tanks and armored personnel carriers in Vietnam often carried a roll of chain link fence which was placed around the vehicle at night to serve as a shield against rocket-propelled grenades. You can model the fence in any scale with wedding veil material, also called tulle. Paint it flat gray. I buy tulle at a local chain store, Minnesota Fabrics, and I assume it's sold by most other fabric stores. *Glenn Kreinus*

Expert panels. I like to use a Waldron punch-and-die set to enhance instrument panels, but it's a difficult tool to use accurately. Here's how I achieve more precision.

If the kit has an instrument-panel decal, photocopy the decal on clear acetate. Punch a hole in the acetate for each instrument, then paint the acetate black. White glue a piece of clear acetate to the back of the punched piece. Glue this assembly to the decal with the clear acetate between the

Shade around wheel rims and lug nuts with a technical pen.

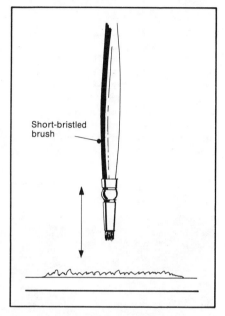

Short-bristled brush

Cast-iron look. To replicate rough cast iron on armored vehicles, apply a liberal coat of liquid cement to the plastic kit parts. While the plastic is still soft, rough up the surface with a small, stiff-bristled brush. Paint and finish the model when the cement is dry.

Dave Doler

Bullet holes. Drill a hole of the desired diameter in the plastic. Using a sharp knife and holding the blade at an angle, scrape a circular depression around the hole. Then sand the rim of the hole lightly. Brush metallic paint around the edge of the hole to replicate bare metal.

Ed Szumlas

black acetate and the decal. If a decal is not provided (or is inadequate), I build the panel with Waldron scale instruments, then follow the same procedure.

Always use acetate specifically designed for a photocopy machine. Any good print shop or stationery store will advise you — especially if you are using their copier! Remember, not all copiers reproduce at exactly 100 percent. To test the accuracy of a copier, check a copy against the original.

Matthew MacKay

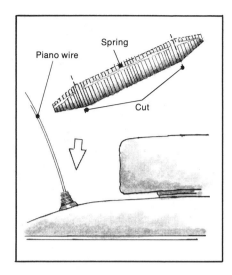

Tank antenna. To create realistic antenna mounts, I use the spring from empty disposable lighters. These springs taper at either end, so I cut off about four coils with nippers, then glue this to the vehicle. Next I super glue a piano-wire antenna into the center of the coil. Add white glue to the base to blend everything together.

Alvin E. Hubert

Easy graffiti. Typewriter correction paper makes good-looking chalk graffiti. Tape the correction paper to the tank, bomb, or wall, and write your message with the blunt end of a needle or with a sharp pencil. After removing the paper, spray on clear finish to seal the message.

Walt Walko

Bomb graffiti. Add a final touch of realism to models by applying graffiti to the bombs they carry. Appropriately worded sentiments can be added with a white pencil, which creates the proper chalked-on look.

Will Reynolds

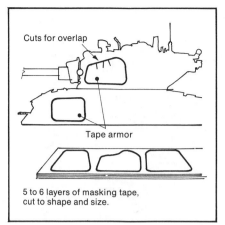

Appliqué armor. Need appliqué armor on a model tank? Lay five or six layers of masking tape on a piece of glass and cut to the shape of the armor panels with a sharp blade. Then simply peel up the panel and stick it onto the model. If you need to go around a compound curve, you may have to cut little "v"s out of the edges.

Melvin Mays

Scale maps. Need scale maps for an airplane cockpit or diorama? Cut them out of a pilot's equipment catalog. They're printed in color on thin paper and look great folded and placed on the seat or in a pilot's lap. You'll also find charts and placards that can be used. See aviation magazines for addresses.

Robert Heffner Jr.

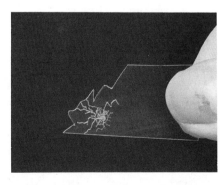

Scale glass. An inexpensive and safe way to simulate windows or broken glass is to use artist's acetate. It comes in a variety of thicknesses and sheet sizes. You can simulate cracks by scribing with a sharp knife. Look for acetate in art-supply stores.

Bill Wells

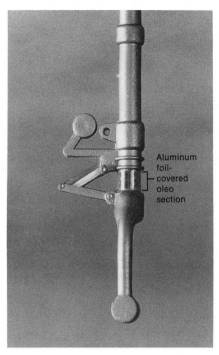

Oleo struts. To detail oleo struts on aircraft landing gear, you could replace the plastic oleo section with a piece of chrome tubing. The easier way is to glue a piece of aluminum foil to the section and trim away the excess. I use Bare-Metal Foil since it already has an adhesive on it. [See *Sources*, page 48.] Burnish the foil with a cotton swab. It's easy to hide the seam behind the "scissors" of the strut.

Paul Boyer

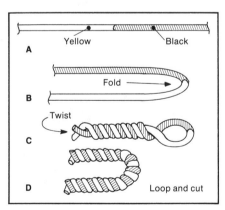

Ejection rings. To model aircraft ejection-seat handles, paint one half of a length of copper wire yellow, the other half black. When the paint dries, fold the wire in half; twist it gently to avoid scratching the paint. Loop the twisted wire into the desired size of the ejection ring, cut excess wire, and super glue the loop.

Craig Baldwin

Wires and conduits. Electrical wires, conduits, hydraulic lines, and fuel lines can be simulated with several diameters of solder, available in hardware and electrical supply stores.

Tim Cislo

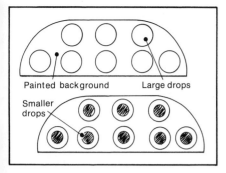

Painless panels. Here's how to paint light-colored borders on instrument panels. First, paint the overall background color. Next, apply large dots of the color you want the instrument border to be. Apply a slightly smaller dot of darker paint for the instrument itself. This is easier than trying to paint the tiny, raised rim of the instrument border.

Paul Adams

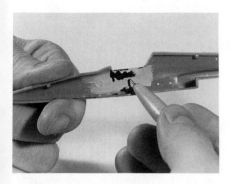

Draw in cockpit detail. To add detail to the sidewalls of 1/72 scale aircraft cockpits, draw it in with a razor point pen such as Pilot or Nikko. Squares, rectangles, and lines can simulate the various boxes and plumbing found in the sidewall area. Add small dots of color to represent fuses, switches, and knobs.

Although it is two-dimensional, this effect is convincing when it's viewed through a stock kit canopy.

Will Reynolds

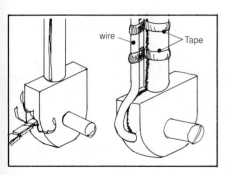

Aircraft brake lines. Black metal wire makes good brake lines for aircraft. Use a pin vise or a hot wire to make a hole in the strut. Super glue the wire in place, and wrap small strips of tape around the strut to hold the line in position.

Marvin Howell

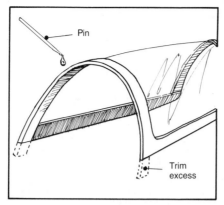

Lead foil canopy frames. An advantage of vacuum-formed aircraft canopies is their in-scale thinness. But the frame around the inside edges of the real thing is usually visibly thicker than the glass. Lead foil replicates this frame well.

Ask a dentist if you can have the lead foil inserts that are discarded from bite-wing X-ray plates: They're thinner than lead foil from other sources. Use a steel rule to guide you when you cut the foil. A tiny bit of super glue is enough to attach the foil to the canopy.

James R. McCartney

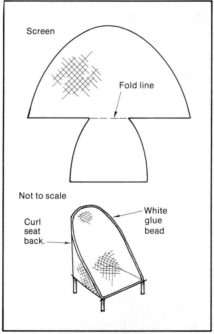

Wicker seats. Many World War I aircraft had wicker seats for the crew members; wicker is lighter than solid wood or metal. Wicker seats can be simulated by making them from fine brass screen [see *Sources*, page 48] using the pattern above. Curl the seat back by bending the screen over the proper size dowel, then fold the seat and glue it with super glue or epoxy.

After the glue has set, run a bead of white glue or epoxy around the edges to simulate the cane framework. Add stretched sprue legs and paint.

Joe Gianfrancesco

A better idea for instruments. The trusty method of scratchbuilding instrument panels is to sandwich a pre-drilled panel, clear plastic sheet, and backing panel that has the instrument faces scribed into the black paint. Instead of using clear plastic sheet, try plastic food wrap. It's much thinner and just as glossy.

Mike Whye

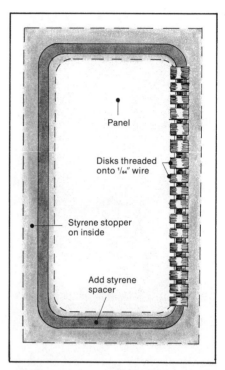

Making aircraft doors. Here's a way to make hinged aircraft doors and hatches. I did this to a 1/24 scale Focke Wolfe Fw 190.

Start with a surgical needle (about 15 cm long, not stainless). The diameter of the needle is 1/32" on the outside, 1/64" on the inside. File the needle into 1/32" disks. Make the disks smooth, then thread them onto 1/64" wire. In most cases you'll end up using 25-35 disks per hinge).

Cut out the panel that is to be hinged. Smooth the rough edges and glue a strip of styrene onto the panel edge to fill the gap created by the cutting. File the side the hinge goes on, leaving about a 1/32" gap for clearance. A strip of styrene must be attached to the inside of the opening to stop the door from swinging inward. Test fit the door and hinge, using tape (on the inside surface) to hold the hinge in position.

Use a needle to place a *tiny* drop of super glue between the disk and the wall, taking care not to clog the whole hinge. Alternate from one end of the hinge to the other to avoid disturbing this delicate assembly. When you've finished on the outside, remove the tape and repeat the procedure from the other side.

Richard Krah

Epoxy lenses. Five-minute epoxy mixed with a dab of red or green paint makes realistic navigation lenses and anti-collision beacons. Just mix up a small batch of five-minute epoxy and a drop of color. With a toothpick, apply a little at a time until you get the size lens you want. (For a large beacon on top of the fuselage, you must make a platform to keep the epoxy from spreading.) Then turn the model upside down, being careful not to let it drip or run to either side.

If the epoxy starts to drip, turn the model back over. The epoxy will set up quickly, so you don't have to keep this up all night. The result is a translucent, shiny lens. For small, clear lenses, the epoxy will bead naturally. This method doesn't work for flush landing lights, however. One last note — to ensure a flawless finish, don't touch the lens for 24 hours.

Rusty White

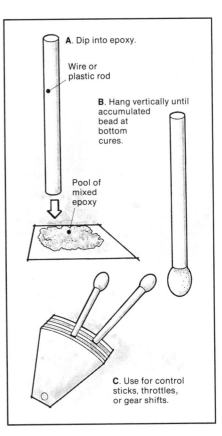

A. Dip into epoxy.

Wire or plastic rod

B. Hang vertically until accumulated bead at bottom cures.

Pool of mixed epoxy

C. Use for control sticks, throttles, or gear shifts.

Wood grain. Simulate the wood grain on a wooden propeller with shoe polish. First paint the prop tan. When it is dry, apply ordinary brown shoe polish with either a shoeshine brush or an old toothbrush. Keep applying the polish until you achieve the shade you want. Wipe off any excess polish with a tissue. Seal it with clear enamel or lacquer.

David Longe

Epoxy knobs. Try using five-minute epoxy to make knobs on control sticks. First, cut all the control sticks you need out of wire or plastic rod, then whip up a small batch of epoxy. Dip each stick into the epoxy, then hang them vertically until the epoxy sets. The epoxy will run down and accumulate at the end, forming a smooth knob.

Mark Savage

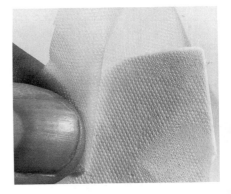

Stretch-formed visor. If you're dissatisfied with the look of the visors on pilot figures, here's a way to make your own visors. All you need is clear plastic (check your hobby store). Shave the old visor from the helmet, and cut the helmet to the shape it would be without the visor. Cut a strip of clear plastic, heat it, and stretch form it around the helmet (1). After the plastic has cooled you can remove it and cut it to fit exactly (2); smooth the edges with sandpaper. Paint the inside of the visor gloss black and attach it with white glue (3). I haven't had any trouble with 1/72 scale visors, and if you go bigger than that you may even be able to make movable visors!

Andrzej Antoniuk

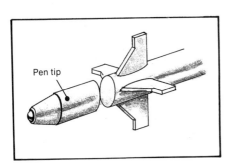

Sidewinder nose. Use the tip of a ball point pen to fabricate the front of a Sidewinder missile in 1/72 scale. A ⅛″ section can be grafted onto the forward section of kit-supplied missiles, or onto tubing for scratchbuilt missiles.

Gary Chambers

Pen tip

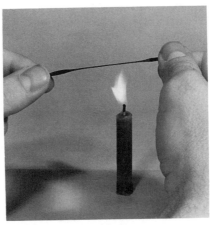

Stretched strut stock. Large styrene strut stocks can be stretched like sprue to form smaller struts. When stretched, the strut stock retains its airfoil shape. This is perfect to replace the outsize struts provided in some small-scale biplane kits.

Paul Boyer

Diamond texture pattern. I found plastic packaging material wrapped around glassware that had a texture similar to that found on interior panels in helicopters and on nonskid panels on armored vehicles. I attempted to bond this .001″ material to sheet styrene with liquid glue, but it wouldn't stick; polyethylene is resistant to most adhesives. But the liquid glue softened the styrene enough to produce an impression of the sheet's pattern on its surface. The result is ready-to-use sheet styrene with a diamond grid pattern.

Alan Ernat

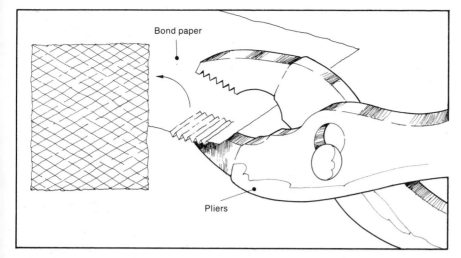

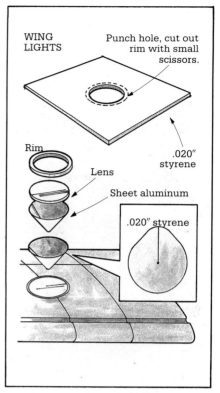

Cockpit walls. Replicate the quilted-fabric covering on cockpit walls by embossing heavy white paper stock with pliers. *Jon Lopez*

Shrink tubing "pipes." Heat-shrink tubing is used in electronics to cover soldered connections. When heated, the tube shrinks to a tight fit. It also works well in models for replicating cylindrical objects (like an auto exhaust pipe). It's malleable, takes paint, and is inexpensive. Shrink tubing can be found at any electronics store. *Mark Allman*

Bullet holes. Hold a needle with a pliers, heat the needle, and push the needle through the plastic at an angle a bullet would be likely to take. Remove the needle quickly. Trim the raised lip around each bullet hole with a knife and touch silver paint around the edges to replicate chipped paint. A coat of flat softens the silver to a believable sheen.

Greg Hildebrandt

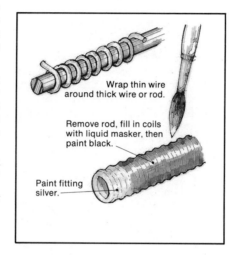

Oxygen hose. Wrap thin wire around thicker wire in a loose spiral, then coat the coiled wire with liquid mask. When the mask dries, paint the "hose" and bend it to shape. Paint a fitting on one end and attach the other end of the hose to a regulator made of stretched sprue. *Bob Steinbrunn*

Wing lights. Here's a handy way to make realistic wing lights with reflectors.

You'll need a single-hole paper punch, small scissors, scrap .020″ styrene sheet, clear acetate, aluminum sheet from a disposable pie pan or frozen food container, five-minute epoxy, and liquid plastic cement.

Step 1: Use the paper punch to make a hole in the .020″ styrene, then cut around the edge of the hole to form the rim.

Step 2: Make a receptacle by cutting out an egg-shaped piece of .020″ styrene slightly larger than the rim. Make a single cut from the narrow end to the center. Shape the piece into a cone and glue the overlapping edges with liquid plastic cement. Sand the top of the cone until it fits snugly against the rim.

Step 3: Make a reflector by repeating Step 2, but this time use the aluminum sheet from a disposable pie pan or frozen food container (ordinary aluminum foil is too flimsy). Attach the reflector to the receptacle with a drop of five-minute epoxy.

Step 4: Punch a lens from clear acetate and glue it to the rim with five-minute epoxy.

Ron Lowry

Scotch Decorator tape. If you need thin tape in colors such as red, yellow, blue, and green, try Scotch Decorator tape, sold in ½″-wide rolls and packaged in familiar 3M dispensers.

This is a dime store item that's hard to find except during the winter holiday season, so buy a year's supply at a time.

Burr Angle

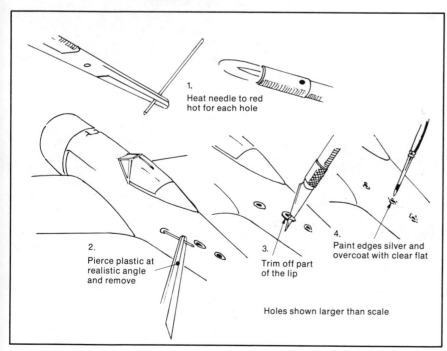

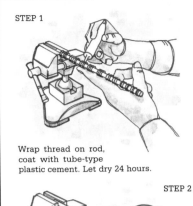

STEP 1

Wrap thread on rod,
coat with tube-type
plastic cement. Let dry 24 hours.

STEP 2

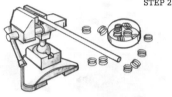

Cut the thread between coils with a single-edge razor blade or hobby knife and slide the coils off the rod.

STEP 3

Place the coils inside the boat and coat each with liquid plastic cement.

Rope coils. Obtain a metal rod several inches long and about 1/4" in diameter. Mount the rod horizontally in a vise. Wrap the rod with spirals of carpet thread, forming coils about 1/8" long. Tie off the loose end of the thread. Liberally coat the coils with tube-type plastic cement and let dry for at least 24 hours. Cut the thread between the coils with a single-edge razor blade or hobby knife, and gently slide the coils off the rod. They'll be rigid and won't look very good. Don't despair; they're supposed to look like that for now.

Pick up a coil with tweezers and place it on the model in an appropriate location. A crochet hook or knitting needle makes it easy to hold a coil in place. Now coat the coil with liquid plastic cement. The coil will immediately loosen, falling into position realistically. This is one of my standard techniques; you can use it for all sorts of dioramas, as well as ship models.

Les Wilkins

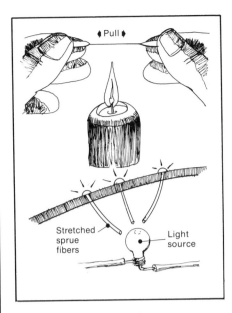

Pull

Stretched sprue fibers Light source

Homemade fiber optics. It's possible to make optical fibers from stretched sprue. Use clear runners from canopies or windshields. Heat the clear rods over a candle until they soften, then pull the ends apart. The faster and farther you pull, the thinner the strands that are stretched. Thicker strands will show more light, while thin strands can be curved tighter. The resulting strands can be used as optical fibers to transmit light from a light source to the tip of the fiber. These fibers are great for lighting effects in boxed dioramas and spacecraft.

Vincent Wong

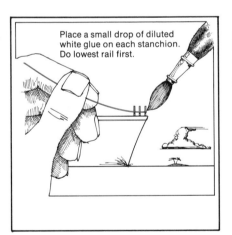

Place a small drop of diluted white glue on each stanchion. Do lowest rail first.

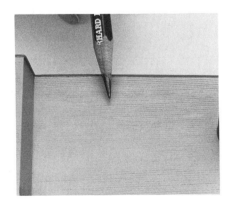

Tiny oxygen hoses. There are commercially available oxygen hoses to detail large-scale models, but for small scales you have to improvise. I use the filaments from burned-out light bulbs. Here's how: First, wrap the bulb in a rag — one that you don't want to keep. Then break the bulb with a hammer and use a tweezers to fish through the shards for the filament. This is not a project for youngsters — the broken glass is extremely thin and sharp. Handle the fragile filament with care.

After you've wrapped up the rag with the broken bulb inside and thrown it away, dip the filament in black paint. The paint will fill the space in between the coils, producing a realistic miniature hose. The filament can also be sprayed black, leaving the center unfilled to represent coiled intercom lines.

Paul Boyer

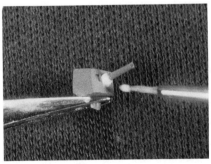

Ship details. Make ship railings from clear stretched sprue. Practice on the main deck until you get the hang of it: The rails are relatively straight there. Start with the lowest rail. Using a 0000 brush, apply thinned white glue to the first bow stanchion and touch the end of the sprue to the white glue.

Paint white glue onto the face of the gun shield and around the gun barrel to form a blast bag.

You can easily get the effect of cracks between deck planks by grazing raised details with the side of a soft lead pencil. Although it looks shiny after it is applied, it will look just right after a sealer coat of clear flat.

Dennis Moore

Preston Russell

5. Dioramas and Displays

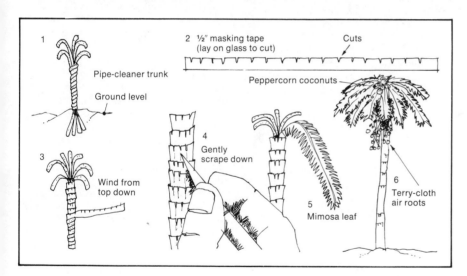

Foam-core board. Foam-core board is expanded styrene with a paper or plastic facing. Brands such as Monsanto's Fome-Cor and Amoco's Artcor are sold in many thicknesses in sizes up to 4' x 8'. Most art-supply stores stock a good selection. The material is rigid, lightweight, and easy to cut. It's great for structure walls, display cases, photo backdrops, and runways.

Burr Angle

Get down low. Photographs of models are interesting when they're photographed at simulated eye level. Wind down your tripod until the center of the lens is five or six scale feet above whatever surface the model is resting on.

Burr Angle

Palm trees. Make a realistic palm tree trunk by winding masking-tape strips onto an armature of pipe cleaners. Before wrapping, slice tiny crosscuts along the top edge of the masking tape about 1/8" apart. After wrapping, scrape downward with a sharp blade to make the top edge of the tape curl down. Paint the trunk buff and apply a dark wash.

The palm fronds are sections of mimosa leaf dipped in polyurethane and glued to the hooked-over ends of the pipe-cleaner trunk. Airbrush the leaves flat green. Simulate the air roots at the top with bits of terry cloth that have been picked apart, and add coconuts made of peppercorns.

Jon Clemens

Landscaping material. For landscaping, I use insulating foam sealant, available at hardware stores. (One brand is "Great Stuff.") I use waxed paper for a working surface. The foam can be affixed with white glue, it takes paint well, and the texture is great. Use a stick of ice to shape the foam after it is dispensed. Some words of caution: The foam is potentially hazardous; *read the directions*! Also, since the foam becomes rigid and it's hard to clean up, it doesn't store well. I recommend one application per can.

Denzil Coppler

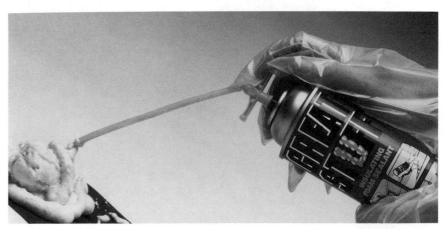

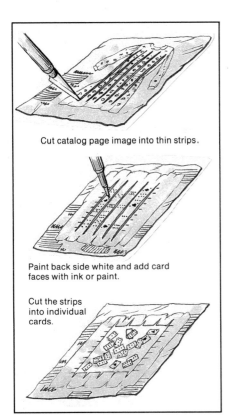

Cut catalog page image into thin strips.

Paint back side white and add card faces with ink or paint.

Cut the strips into individual cards.

Diorama details. You can use catalog pictures of wallpaper and fabrics as wallpaper, draperies, and rugs in dioramas. Make playing cards by cutting small pieces from these pictures, painting the reverse side white, and carefully painting the faces with red and black paint or ink.

Bruce Culver

Making waves. In his out-of-print book *The Colonial Schooner* Harold Hahn suggests modeling waves on a 3/4" sheet of Lucite. Use a motor tool with an egg-shaped steel burr. Scoop out waves, moving your hand in the same direction as the "current." Mix blue-green acrylic with matte medium for a semigloss finish. *Anthony Santos*

Foam functions. Plastic-foam forms found in computer or stereo boxes make good assembly and painting jigs, as well as protecting shipped models.

Robert J. Rohrback

Model storage boxes. Looking for boxes that protect your models from dust, dirt, and the cat, yet are strong enough to stack without collapsing? Check out the rigid, clear plastic boxes designed for shoe and sweater storage, available at department stores such as K mart. Prices range from $1 to $5. The shoe boxes are ideal for small 1/72 scale aircraft or 1/35 scale armor; the large sweater boxes hold medium-size models or small dioramas.

Dave Musikoff

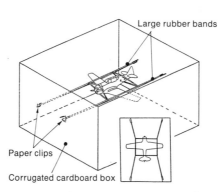

Large rubber bands

Paper clips

Corrugated cardboard box

No broken pieces. Use a stiff corrugated cardboard box, paper clips, and rubber bands to make a container to transport models. First, use a pushpin to make holes for the paper clips, then stretch the rubber bands between the paper clips. Additional bands may be run perpendicular to the main bands for more support. Several models may be carried in the same box by careful placement of the main bands.

I work on offshore oil rigs and most of my travel is via crew boats, which can be rough. I've transported my models dozens of times with this system and have yet to break a part! *Wade Tyler*

Snowbound dioramas. Tired of making a mess of snowy dioramas with cornstarch, sugar, or flour? Try mixing equal portions of white glue and a water-soluble white paint and applying it to your base. Wait till it's tacky, then scatter clear glitter on top. As the mixture dries, a sparkling surface appears.

For a windblown snow effect, place the "wintered" diorama base in a microwave oven for 15 to 30 seconds on full power. The result is a rippled, wavy surface that looks like drifted snow. Make sure you don't cook any plastic models, or they will take on a rippled, wavy appearance too!

David V. Chevalier

Dramatic diorama photos. Here is a simple way to depict bomb blasts in photos of a diorama. Paint the blast on clear glass, set the glass in front of the scene, and shoot the photo through the glass. Use a polarized lens filter to avoid glare or reflections in the glass.

Koyu Go

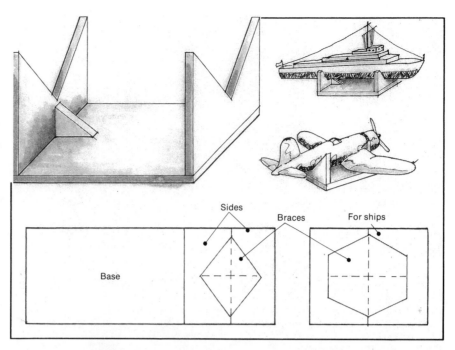

Transporting models. We asked Joe Gianfrancesco to ship a completed model to FSM for a photo session. Joe lived in Salt Lake City, and was faced with the problem of sending a delicate aircraft model all the way to Milwaukee. His solution? He found a flat-sided plastic foam box (a lot like a six-pack cooler) a few inches larger in all dimensions than the model. Then he lined the box with small blocks of foam rubber and polyurethane seat-cushion material. He cut other blocks to support the plane by its wing tips and horizontal stabilizer tips. More blocks went between the tops of the wing and horizontal stabilizer tips and the top of the box. The blocks were slightly compressed when Joe put on the lid, ensuring the model could not shift. He sealed the lid with filament tape.

The plane survived a 1,455-mile journey with absolutely no damage, and because the packaging materials are reusable, we packed the model in them when we returned it.

Burr Angle

Water, water everywhere. Use Elmer's Tub & Tile Caulking for water on ship diorama bases. It squirts from a tube like toothpaste and can be spread into wave patterns with a wet finger. Let it dry for 24 hours before painting. Finish with a coat of clear gloss varnish to give the waves a wet look.

Ed Wojcik

Model stand. Here's a piece of equipment I used for building rockets, but have found useful for building, painting, moving, and even displaying aircraft and ship models. I use 1/2 mm- to 1 mm-thick balsa or plastic about half again as long as the finished base. Simply cut the material as shown, glue together, and you'll have a handy stand or jig.

Eric McCann

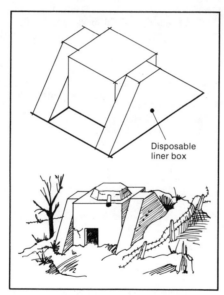

Easy structures. The box that baby-bottle liners come in is vacuum-formed plastic. Inverted, it looks like a concrete bunker, about 12′ tall in 1/72 scale. Add a door and viewing slits, paint and texture it to look like cement, and it's ready for camouflage. I've found computer equipment and toys packaged in similar containers.

Glenn Abramczyk

Budget dirt. Spray a diorama base the desired color, letting the paint build up, then sprinkle dirt on the wet paint. Let it dry, then lightly spray over the area once more to seal it. Vary the dirt to create different textures.

Hector Montenegro

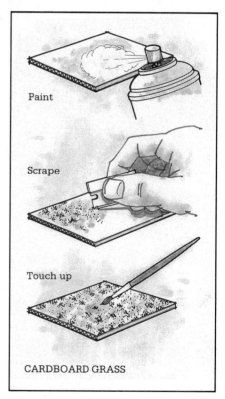

Cardboard grass. Need grass on a diorama? Paint cardboard, then lightly scrape it with the tip of a sharp razor blade. The scraping raises the cardboard fibers, and it creates tiny blades of "grass." Touch up the grass with a brush.

Practice on a piece of scrap and you'll soon get the hang of it. The grass is perfect for 1/48 to 1/32 scale.

Troy Borgerson

Sources

A

Acetate, adhesive backed: Zip-a-Tone, 150 Fencl Lane, Hillside, IL 60162

Activa Products: see *Celluclay*

Aleen's Original Tacky Glue: Artis, Inc., Solvang, CA 93463

American Art Clay Co.: see *Sculptamold*

Auto World: see *Hot knife*

B

Bare-Metal Foil: Bare-Metal Foil & Hobby Co., P. O. Box 82, Farmington, MI 48024

The Biggs Co.: see *A + B Epoxy Putty*

Binney & Smith Inc.: see *Liquitex*

Bostik Blu-Tack: Bostik, Inc., Boston Street, Middleton, MA 01949

Brass screen: LMG Enterprises, 1627 S. 26th St., Sheboygan, WI 53081

Brass sheet, rod, and tubing: K&S Engineering, 6917 W. 59th, Chicago, IL 60638

C

Castolite: Castolite, P. O. Box 391, Woodstock, IL 60098

Celluclay: Activa Products, Inc., Marshall, TX 75670

Chains, scale:
  Campbell Scale Models, c/o Wm. K. Walthers, Inc., P. O. Box 18676, Milwaukee, WI 53218
  Clover House, Box 62D, Sebastopol, CA 95473

Chartpak graphic tape: Chartpak/Pickett, 1 River Road, Leeds, MA 01053-9732

Clip-on sanding disks: Merit Abrasive Products, 201 W. Manville, P. O. Box 5447, Compton, CA 90224

D

DAP, Inc.: see *Duratite*

Detail parts:
  Detail Associates, P. O. Box 5357, San Luis Obispo, CA 93403
  Grandt Line Products, Inc., 1040B Shary Court, Concord, CA 94518

Detail parts, photoetched: see *Photoetched detail parts*

Dremel Moto-Tool and accessories: Emerson Electric Co., P. O. Box 1468, Racine, WI 53401

The Dromedary: see *Photoetched detail parts*

Duratite Surfacing Putty: DAP Inc., Dayton, OH 45401

Durham's Water Putty: Donald Durham Co., P. O. Box 804, Des Moines, IA 50304

E

Emerson Electric: see *Dremel Moto-Tool*

En-Pak: see *Lazy Susan bearings*

Epoxy putty
  A + B Epoxy Putty: The Biggs Co., 612 E. Franklin, El Segundo, CA 90245
  Milliput: Rosemont Hobby Shop, P. O. Box 139, Trexlertown, PA 18087

Evergreen Scale Models: see *Styrene sheet, rod, and strip*

F

The Floating Drydock: see *Photoetched detail parts*

Formaline graphic tape: Graphic Products Corp., 3601 Edison Place, Rolling Meadows, IL 60008

G

Gold Medal Models: see *Photoetched detail parts*

Grandt Line: see *Detail parts*

Graphic tape: see *Chartpak* and *Formaline*

Grip-Rite Cushion Grips: Hoyle Products, 302 Orange Grove, Fillmore, CA 93015

H

"Helping hands" vises:
  K&S Engineering, 6917 W. 59th, Chicago, IL 60638
  PanaVise Products, 2850 E. 29th St., Long Beach, CA 90806

Hot knife: Auto World, 701 N. Keyser Ave., Scranton, PA 18508

K

K&S Engineering: see *Brass sheet, rod, and tubing* and *"Helping hands"*

L

Lazy Susan bearings: En-Pak, 840 E. Lewiston, Ferndale, MI 48220

Liquitex: Binney & Smith Inc., Easton, PA 18042

LMG Enterprises: see *Brass screen*

M

Merit Abrasive Products: see *Clip-on sanding disks*

Micro-files: Woodcraft, 210 Wood County Industrial Park, P. O. Box 1686, Parkersburg, WV 26102-1686

Milliput: Rosemont Hobby Shop, P. O. Box 139, Trexler Mall, Trexlertown, PA 18087

Model airplane control line:
  Perfect Parts Co., 1 N. Haven St., Baltimore, MD 21224
  Sig Manufacturing Co., Inc., 401-7 S. Front St., Montezuma, IA 50171

Model railroad product catalog: Wm. K. Walthers, P. O. Box 18676, Milwaukee, WI 53218

Model Technologies, 2761 Saturn, Unit E, Brea, CA 92621

P

PanaVise Products: see *"Helping hands"*

Perfect Parts Co.: see *Model airplane control line*

Photoetched detail parts:
  The Dromedary, 6324 Belton Drive, El Paso, TX 79912
  The Floating Drydock, c/o General Delivery, Kresgeville, PA 18333
  Gold Medal Models, 12332 Chapman Ave., No. 81, Garden Grove, CA 92640
  Model Technologies, 2761 Saturn, Unit E, Brea, CA 92621
  Waldron Model Products, P. O. Box 431, Merlin, OR 97532

Plastruct: see *Styrene structural forms*

Polyform Products: see *Sculpey*

Punch and die set: Waldron Model Products (address above)

R

Resin casting material: see *Castolite*

Rosemont Hobby Shop: Rosemont Hobby Shop, P. O. Box 139, Trexler Mall, Trexlertown, PA 18087

S

Sculpey Modeling Compound: Polyform Products, 9420 Byron St., Schiller Park, IL 60176

Sculptamold: American Art Clay Co., Inc., 4717 W. 16th St., Indianapolis, IN 46222

Sig Manufacturing Co.: see *Model airplane control line*

Styrene sheet, rod, and strip: Evergreen Scale Models, 12808 N. E. 125th Way, Kirkland, WA 98034

Styrene structural forms: Plastruct, 1020 S. Wallace Place, City of Industry, CA 91748

T

Tacky glue: see *Aleen's Original Tacky Glue*

W

Waldron Model Products, P. O. Box 431, Merlin, OR 97532

Wm. K. Walthers, P. O. Box 18676, Milwaukee, WI 53218

Woodcraft: see *Micro-files*

Z

Zip-a-Tone: see *Acetate*